Scams & Swords

Bear Ursa

"We are never so easily deceived as when we imagine we are deceiving others."
— François de La Rochefoucauld

Chapter 1

Harry Maxwell took a deep breath. The fresh, salty sea air filled his spirits as much as it did his lungs.

Peace, calm and serenity washed over him as the waves washed over the shore. Taking root, feeling the sharp snap of cold metal from his favourite bench—it was older than him by now, paint peeling, specks of rust showing beneath.

Harry sighed, pulling his phone from his pocket, and tapped on the dating app.

Jessica, 24, King's Lynn. Little young, Harry thought, raising an eyebrow at the tagline "casual encounters only".

He didn't have to mull over that unmatch for very long.

"Hi Harry!" Olivia beamed, his heart daring to skip a beat as she manifested beside him, quickly joining him on the bench. His secretary.

"Sorry, you startled me! I was just enjoying the sounds of the sea. Relaxing after work."

Hunstanton was a coastal town in Norfolk, where Harry had moved to after his parents passed away. Fields as far as the eye could see, flat all around, not a hill or mound in sight. His aunt owned a one-bedroom, end-terraced house here—now Harry's responsibility, whilst she sadly withered in a nearby nursing home. Dementia.

He would visit, from time to time. Harry frowned, recalling his last—where she called him Thomas. His dad's name. He sighed. At least she hadn't called him Mary.

A number of his clients suffered the same fate. Dementia and fraud were fast friends, which Harry knew all too well.

Harry shook his head a little, turning to face Olivia. She was standing there staring.

"Right! Sorry, Olivia. Lost in thought. Weren't you going to see some pandas, or something?" Harry asked.

"I was, but saw you! You coming with me, then?"

"I'd best not, Olivia. You go, have some fun. I'll head home—see you in the morning."

Harry rushed to his feet, beginning the slow march home, before stopping at the sight of a familiar face, grinning wide.

"Harry bruv! Nice suit, innit. Buy a guy an ice cream?"

His friend Jester. Aptly named, the bloody clown.

"Really must be going, Jester. Heading home, get out of this tie."

"Come on, bruv! Hang out with your mate for a bit. Come get some ice cream."

Harry grinned as they marched over to the vendor and ordered an ice cream for Jester. He mimicked dropping it on Harry's suit.

"Hey! Not funny!" Harry remarked, though his grin betrayed his words. "You robbed me for ice cream, why not dinner too? I'll make us lasagne?"

"Way too many carbs, bruv! Anyway... Laters!"

Jester sprinted off with his sugary treat. That was a quick hang-out session. Still, Harry smiled despite himself as he walked home, lasagne for one on the menu. At least there would be leftovers to keep the fridge company.

Harry lingered a little longer in the kitchen that evening, gazing at a picture of himself and his aunt. She was already sixty when she took him in, whilst his brother Tim was sent to live with their uncle in Norwich.

Harry stared at his phone for a long while. He sighed, and scrolled through his contacts to his brother.

"Hi Tim, it's just me, Harry. I was just thinking of you. Hope you're having a good day, and looking forward to swords on Thursday? Love, Harry."

Harry pondered over it for a moment. Perhaps it was a little formal? Not like he was asking him to a masked banquet or something. Didn't matter. Harry smiled and hit send anyway.

His gaze turned back to the photo, minutes passing in moments as a text came back.

"Harry mate! Good to hear from you. I sold three cars today, crushing it as usual. I'm looking forward to it lots, I'll crush you, too! Love ya bro, Tim x"

Tim was probably right—years they'd had the hobby, sword fighting as medieval re-enactors, but never once could Harry beat him.

Harry frowned. Tim was a champion in all that he did, happily married with two boys, a loving wife, and top of his game as a car salesman.

Harry yawned, dragging his weary bones up the stairs, gentle creak of the wood announcing his approach to Mr Snuffles, his childhood stuffed rabbit—sat beside the pillow, keeping a watchful gaze over Harry as he slept.

Sleep over in a flash, Harry groaned, ears assaulted by the relentlessly cruel tune of "Barbie Girl", from his phone sat on the opposite bedside table.

Just out of reach for him to easily paw it off, and a song that truly irritated him. No easier way to force himself out of bed. Tip from his insightful secretary.

Harry got up, grabbed his phone—resisting the primal urge to drop it in his glass of water with a satisfying plop—and silenced the infernal alarm. Morning routine, tie tightened, off to the office.

Harry smiled as he spotted Olivia at her front desk, already tapping away at her computer. Always here first, always busy.

Harry's hand lingered on the cold glass a moment as he pushed open the door.

"Good morning, Olivia," he said, noticing the fresh scent of strawberries.

"Hi Harry! I got a new perfume. I read something that said the smell of strawberries makes people happy. Are you happy to see me, Harry?"

Harry couldn't help but return her infectious, bubbly smile, his day already improving.

"Oh yes! I noted you're always here first, getting a jump on the day. I admire the spirit. Well, in I go, see what tall tales are told today. See you at lunch."

Chapter 2

"What got you into spamming, exactly? Why stop?"

Harry had asked this question a time or two before. Wasn't his first counselling session with a spammer, nor would it be his last. He'd do his best to help, as always.

"Tell you the truth, it was just easy money, yeah? But my nan clicked on the link I sent out too. She had to sell her favourite bracelet, Harry, just to cover the debts. Opened my eyes."

Harry smiled a little, thinking back to his troubled teens. The McDonald's job, the spamming forums, the guilt. Easy money? Doesn't exist.

"It's easy to detach yourself from your actions from behind a keyboard, isn't it, David?" Harry began, smiling at his former self.

David glared at the floor, clenching his fists. *Preaching to the choir, Harry.*

"Bank wouldn't help her, either. I didn't know it could lead to such big losses, I swear! I thought it was just pennies per person. But nan lost thousands!"

David slammed his fists on the sofa.

Harry looked at his bookshelf. Too many declined claims, too many tears.

"Mr Maxwell?"

"Yes, sorry." Harry met David's eyes. "Well, I must confess, I was exactly where you were, some twenty or so years ago." Harry sighed, pausing a beat.

5

"You can't change what you did, or the consequences associated with those choices. Your future is in your hands, so make better choices. Give your nan my number, I'll try my best to help."

David nodded, facing Harry with a grin, as Harry handed him a book he wrote on scam psychology. Harry hoped he'd actually read it, but sighed a little anyway, watching the kid leave. Maybe he should get a cartoon giraffe drawn on the cover, or something, to make it slightly less unappealing.

Moments later, a buzz from the intercom jolted Harry upright.

"Lunchtime, Harry! I made us both sandwiches. Can I come in?" Olivia announced happily over the intercom.

"Sure. Thanks, Olivia."

The office door creaked open, Olivia rushing inside and closing it behind her.

"I made you tuna today, Harry. Got some in special, just for you!" She beamed with pride, eyes fixed firmly on his reaction.

"Thanks, Olivia." Harry mumbled, taking a bite as he focused his gaze on his emails.

"So there's this film tonight, Harry. Oh and that red panda exhibit I mentioned, too. Do you want to go?" Olivia suggested, voice cracking slightly.

Harry simply shook his head, eyes still glued to his email. Nowhere near appropriate.

"I read your first book, Harry. It was fun! I learned all about pig butchering and sucker lists."

That caught Harry's gaze. Fun wasn't exactly the word he had in mind, but did admire the enthusiasm.

"Yes, cruel really, how they 'fatten the pig' before the 'butchering'. All a bit savage really. Added to lists once they pay up."

Harry squinted a little as Olivia clapped her hands together, bouncing a little in her seat.

He didn't judge. This stuff fascinated him too.

Lunchtime neared its end, Olivia quickly grabbing her Tupperware, standing to leave.

"Well, you've a few more to see today, Harry. I'll get back out there. I'm going to study on the computer between your clients like we discussed, OK?"

Harry nodded and beckoned for her to leave, already back to the emails.

One in particular had caught his eye, shoulders slumping. A declined complaint, no refund for his client. Maybe he needed to add more 'disappointing' to it. Maybe more 'legal action'. Maybe even drop the 'Warm' before 'Regards'. Chilling.

Harry's phone buzzed again. Fumbled for it in his suit jacket, sat in the side pocket.

His dating app. Seems he had another match— Charlotte, 28, English teacher.

Harry smiled on reading her profile, seeing she was keen to date with the intent to marry. But the opening message he received of "hi" didn't exactly move mountains.

Harry pocketed his phone, focus back to his email.

Seconds stretched staring at the wall-mounted analogue clock, tapping his pen against the desk.

Harry jolted upright with a shock—blasted intercom buzzer. He really needed to stop procrastinating and change it for a less intrusive option. Maybe a cattle prod?

"Harry, your next appointment is here a little early. I'll send her in."

Well, back to the grindstone.

Chapter 3

Harry quickly shuffled papers on his desk, then fumbled with the knot of his tie.

The office door creaked open revealing a woman looking to be in her fifties, possibly sixties. Grey hair, short, thin—and wearing that familiar frown.

She slumped on the sofa, staring. Still hadn't spoken, but turned her gaze to the credentials adorning Harry's wall—then his bookcase.

"Susan Mayweather, is that right? Harry Maxwell. Pleasure to meet you, despite the circumstances. Before we begin, you approved transcription on your survey— mind if we go over that?"

She turned to look at him, before quickly fixing her gaze on the floor—offering a small nod.

Harry fumbled in his pocket and produced a small, black plastic device, smooth to the touch.

"So this device uses artificial intelligence to accurately record and transcribe conversations. The transcriptions are only accessible to myself or my secretary, stored securely, and only with your explicit permission. Happy?"

Harry studied her, waiting for a reaction. Her shoulders relaxed and she sighed.

"Susan, that's right. Transcribe away, Harry."

Harry smiled, and pressed in the plastic button with his thumb. One reassuring little click later, and a tiny green light showed recording active.

He had Olivia to thank for this little gem. Harry had about laughed her out of the office when she first suggested new-age artificial intelligence gadgets, but it had been a lifesaver. So much time saved.

"So... I've been struggling, Harry." Susan started, arms once again folded. "I lost a lot of money. All of it, actually. Mine, and my husband's. He's been cruel about the whole thing, and I can't exactly blame him for it, can I? I'm an idiot."

Her voice cracked as tears welled in her eyes.

Harry nodded, placing his hands on the desk, smooth to the touch.

"I read your survey—the notorious whiskey barrel scam. I'll skip the part you're sick of hearing, and won't tell you I'm sorry that happened to you," Harry began.

A slight grin formed on Susan's face.

"I'm going to start by admonishing you for calling yourself an idiot. It's a true pet peeve of mine, honestly. Nearly every person I counsel says the same thing—I'm an idiot, a moron, a gullible buffoon—well, you're not."

Harry adjusted his tie and took a sip of water before continuing.

"You contend with the forces of organised crime. Trained psychologists, much like myself, working to build scripts and scenarios designed to separate the honest from their earnings. Other side of the coin, if you will."

Susan leaned forward a little, brief smile flickering beneath the surface.

"If not a fool then, Mr Psychologist, what am I?"

Her expression hardened, her smile a challenge, her eyes fixed firmly on his throat.

"A victim."

Susan's smile faded as quickly as it appeared, slumping back in her chair.

"It isn't fair, Harry. I'm so careful, not even remotely gullible. I did everything, I checked Companies House for the company registration, I called the number on the website, it all looked so real." Susan began.

"All those reviews on their Facebook page, all five stars, all made a fortune. But it was a lie, a trick, a scam. All of it. Finally found a way to afford a holiday. I've never even left Norfolk, Harry. Doubt I ever will now."

Might as well try and cheer her up. What could go wrong, Harry thought.

"Well, we're not far from Cambridgeshire. You could drive over, then you'd have at least left Norfolk, right?"

Susan glared at Harry, just for a moment—then relaxed and mustered a brief laugh.

That was lucky. Good job she had a sense of humour.

Susan wiped her cheek and relaxed her shoulders.

"That's exactly my Paul's sense of humour. Well, it was before all this whiskey barrel business."

"So. I see you've tried reporting it to the bank, but didn't really get anywhere. I can take a crack at it, five percent if I win?"

Susan leaned forward in her chair, spark returning to her eyes.

"Oh please, Harry. If there's a chance or a hope that you can help me, please."

Harry stood, reaching out his hand.

"I'll get to work and be in touch in due course. Take care."

Harry smiled, gesturing her towards the door. Pressing the transcription device off.

Olivia pushed open the door with a creak. She awkwardly shuffled backwards holding something, but Harry didn't need to guess what it was. The warm, inviting aroma of melted cheese, baked dough and tomato sauce poked at his nose.

"Pizza time! Margherita, your favourite!" Olivia announced proudly, beaming a smile.

"Oh yes! That's great, Olivia. One of my favourites, in fact, quite right. Thank you. "

Harry gestured for her to drop the box on the desk. She happily complied, then pulled it open.

Olivia sat close, stank of strawberry.

"Harry, I was reading more of your books. Is it really true? Are there scammers who are slaves?"

Harry nodded gently.

"Afraid so, Olivia. There are countries where compounds exist, citizens sold lies by the dozen. They are promised a high-profile IT job in a western country, then redirected to these compounds—identification stolen, whips used for compliance if they don't meet their scamming targets. Sometimes, they're even state-sanctioned."

Olivia frowned, gaze fixed on Harry, but wandering to his tie.

"That tie looks tight, I'll come adjust it."

Olivia happily skipped back to her seat, firmly fixing her gaze on Harry once more, after fiddling with his tie.

"Um, by state-sanctioned, you mean the government lets them do it? But why don't they stop it?"

"Afraid so. Good money in it, sadly."

"Your tie is still looking tight. I'll come adjust it again."

Before she could, Harry simply removed it and unbuttoned the top button of his shirt, Olivia rolling her eyes.

"All better," Harry said as she glared.

"You have no more clients due today, Harry. Should we close up? I was eyeing up an exhibit on penguins at the sea life centre—your favourite animal! Let's go?"

Harry shook his head.

"Not for me, sorry. I've still some work to do here. But you go with your friends, and give the penguins a little wave from me. Do love to watch the little guys waddle."

Olivia frowned briefly.

"I will! I'll get you lots of pictures. See you later, Harry!"

Chapter 4

Harry grinned, glaring at his email client as the white, beaming light glared right back.

Harry tapped away at his keyboard, skilfully crafting a letter of complaint. It was effortless, simple, methodical—why couldn't the dating app be the same?

He sighed as he hit send, reaching for the phone burning a hole in his pocket. *Harry, your subscription has expired.*

There were probably cheaper ways to pay for misery? Why not book that root canal instead? Still, in for a penny, in for more fantastic dates.

This app had a handy feature for subscribers. If a user swiped left, they could leave a comment about why. Couldn't be any worse than the comments after his first school play.

"Nerd."

"What century are you from?"

"Can't even see your face!"

Well, maybe a photo in armour wasn't great. Couldn't see his face, though he didn't consider it much to look at. Might have to bite the bullet and ask his younger brother for some tips. Sold cars, could sell him, Harry thought.

Remaining pizza stuffed in the fridge, Turn of his key in the lock and Harry was out the door.

The fresh, salty sea air soon filled his lungs once more, savouring it a while. Having made his way back to the promenade, he hunted down his familiar, friendly metal bench, eager to feel the sharp snap of cold as he sat once more.

The sea held secrets. Still, something about being sat across from it, the rhythmic sounds of the waves crashing against the shore, the hungry caws of the gulls as they hunted for unguarded chips—Harry was at peace. At home.

"Hi Harry!"

Harry jolted awake, almost lost at sea. Bugger.

Olivia stood beside him, hands behind her back.

"Ah, sorry Olivia. I was relaxing by the sea. Weren't you looking at penguins?"

Olivia came and sat next to him, strawberries back in full force.

"Decided against it. I'll see them next time. Unless you want to come with me? We could discuss your next book."

Harry did consider it; the feedback would be valuable. But Harry could already picture the gazes, the whispers, the leers—real or imagined, they forbade it all the same.

"Not for me, Olivia. I'm seeing my brother and the others tonight."

Olivia bounced a little on the bench.

"You have a brother! What's he like? What's his name? Is he a looker like you, Harry?"

Harry's calm, peace and serenity had washed out to sea, carried away by the same waves that brought it. Perhaps he should just tie his tongue, get it over with.

"Ah, sorry. I got a bit personal, didn't I? I'm sure you have plenty to do, Olivia. Are you meeting your friends here?"

Olivia crossed her arms and glared at the sea.

"No."

Harry shrugged, taking to his feet.

"Well, off home. See you tomorrow."

"Bye, Harry!"

Harry smiled as he set off for home once more, gulls cawing overhead. Almost wished he had some chips to feed them himself.

Chapter 5

Harry tapped away on the steering wheel as he focused on the drive to the church, kit bag in the boot. It seemed fitting, almost biblical that a church was the chosen venue for sword practice. The echoing clang of steel on steel, metal scraping against metal, rang out in the hallowed halls like a church choir.

Turned in, seeing Simon's van sat near the door, open, kit bags ready to be hauled inside. He stood like a sentinel, arms folded, gazing at Harry as he exited his car.

"Harry," Simon declared.

Man of few words, but when he spoke, you listened.

"Good to see you, Simon," Harry began, struggling with his kit bag.

Simon grabbed it from Harry, effortlessly holding it in one hand. The kind of strength and musculature that came from years of hard, practised craft as a lorry mechanic.

Simon was already wearing his chainmail from work that day. He'd started wearing it to his job years ago—the weight overbearing at first, as he struggled to change tyres and fix suspensions, weighed down by the heavy metal. His colleagues laughed initially—but through Simon's stoic, patient work, now effortless.

"Harry, bruv! How's my guy then? Still getting scammed or whatever it is that you do?" Jester mocked, patting Harry on the shoulder.

"Good to see you too, Jester. Still unemployed and pestering your mates for ice cream?"

Jester scowled. "Hey not cool man, I'm going through some stuff.."

Harry frowned, and patted Jester on the shoulder. Ice cream was plenty cool, he thought.

"Sorry. Still working on my sense of humour. No Tim?"

Amusingly, and almost prophetically, Tim pulled into the car park moments later, met with chuckles from the group—even Simon.

"OK Harry, I'll give you that. That was funny. We're cool, innit."

Jester patted Harry on the back, as Tim stepped out of the car, surveying their faces.

"Alright boys! Harry mate, good to see you. What's so funny?"

Jester stepped forwards, arms outstretched, gesturing for a hug.

Harry tingled with anticipation, eagerly awaiting his turn.

"You had to be here, bruv. Harry's a stand-up comic now. Funny stuff—and I ain't just talking about his ugly mug!"

Tim raised an eyebrow, quickly shrugging it off, hauling his kit bag from the boot of his car.

"Open up then, Harry mate," he said.

Harry hurriedly fumbled for the large, iron key in his pocket, then quickly jammed it into the huge, ancient oak doors.

The ancient oak creaked loudly, foreshadowing their presence with an echo through the hallowed halls of the church. Hauling kit bags to the front, they prepared themselves for battle.

Harry felt the cold, smooth steel of his helm beneath his fingers, smiling wide. *Nerd.*

Harry shook his head and fastened his pauldrons, greaves attached and gauntlets following suit. Heart pulsed in his ears.

"Alright boys, I'm fighting with Simon first. Watch the master at work."

Jester drew his short swords, spinning them gracefully in his hands. The arrogance was earned, his skill and speed matched only by the power and patience of Simon.

Simon wielded a mighty, elaborate zweihander. Two metres of solid steel, huge even in the hands of the behemoth himself. His effortless swings as he brought it down, around, sweeping in arcs—Harry gazing in awe.

The two knights circled one another, Tim standing at hand to marshal.

"I want a clean fight, mates. I'm talking to you, Jester."

Simon smirked.

"Come on, bruv! Just announce it already. Let me at him."

Tim raised his sword, sky high, to the roof of the church and the Gods above.

"Lay on arms!"

Jester was merciless. The second Tim spoke, he furiously and relentlessly assaulted Simon.

His blows were met, blocked, and parried with practised precision. Metal scraped against metal, echoing biblically through the church, as the brothers watched in awe. Fight continued as the clangs echoed around them, every blow, every block, one moment away from victory or defeat. Harry's ears rang as Simon's blade rose to block a feint from Jester's right, but his left was already arcing low. Simon twisted, catching the blade on his guard rail, steel screeching as he swept both blades aside.

They started to tire, breathing heavily, panting deep. Simon took a huge, sweeping arc towards Jester, which he nimbly dodged, striking Simon on the pauldron.

"Fight!" Tim declared, sword once again raised to the heavens above.

They embraced, Harry applauding.

"Honestly, nothing Tim or I can do will top that. Might as well pack up and go to the pub." Harry grinned as he stood from the pew, helm heavy under his arm.

"Well, sounds to me like someone's scared, mate. Tired of getting thrashed?"

Bad move, Tim. Time to duel.

The brothers affixed their helms, Simon stood marshal nearby, arms folded.

"Now boys, I know you're brothers, but try to remember it's just for fun, yeah?" Jester said, grin on his face, helmet under his arm.

Harry and Tim circled one another, broadswords at the ready, Harry's breaths short and sharp.

"Lay on arms!" Jester raised his blades, signalling the fight to begin.

Tim brought his blade low, skilfully sweeping for Harry's leg. He came close, knowing full well leg blocks were Harry's weakness. Harry breathed harder, circling again, sword brought up and aiming for Tim's head.

The bout continued for some time, both brothers panting, gasping, circling. Harry took a gambit, a wide arcing swing for Tim's arm—but the familiar thunk of steel on his thigh stopped him halfway.

"That's a wrap! Well done boys!"

Jester applauded, Simon nodding in approval. The brothers hugged, arms around each other, steel clanking against steel as they panted and heaved.

"Skillful," Simon stated simply.

"Harry mate," Tim began, having caught his quickly fleeing breath. "You came bloody close today. You know, man of your height, you might benefit from a longsword—give you that bit of bonus reach?"

Ever the salesman, Harry thought, be it swords or cars—but perhaps he had a point.

"You boys are catching up quick, innit."

Jester put his arms around them, as they all sat on the pew, eager for a break. All save for Simon, once more practising his form.

"Well boys, couple more rounds, then what do you say? Pub?"

Harry and Tim looked at one another, both grinning.

"Let's do it," Harry said, as he prepared for his next bout. Didn't imagine he'd win this one either, but he'd keep trying. Not like he'd lose an arm over it.

Chapter 6

"Alright, brothers in steel. First round's on Simon."

Jester carefully brought a tray over to their table, four pints carefully balanced atop it.

Harry took the glass—and raised it over to Simon, smiling.

"Cheers," Simon stated, downing half his pint in one fell swoop.

Jester turned his chair backwards, sat atop it with legs either side, facing the table.

"Brothers in steel!" he roared, raising his glass.

"Brothers in steel!" they all chimed in, drawing some pointed gazes from pub patrons. *Nerd.*

"Harry mate. You've not been round in a bit, why don't you come Sunday roast? My Yvette's a bloody good cook, mate. Why I married her. Well, and her cracking tits."

Bloody hell. Rude, but honest. Harry couldn't help but grin.

"Besides, boys miss their uncle. Think on it. You're always welcome, mate. Family."

Harry stared at the liquor on the top shelf. Did love spending time with family, but the thought tightened his chest.

Everything changed when the plane crashed, claiming his parents both. Harry closed his eyes, swallowing hard. Sleep would elude him again tonight, no doubt. Oh well, could practise that saxophone again, piss off the neighbours.

Harry sighed. It was a rock and a hard place. Wanted the warmth, but the more time he spent there, the more he missed what wasn't his.

"Oi Tim, can I come too? Promise I'll behave myself around your missus," Jester said with exaggerated innocence.

"Wind your neck in, mate. Next round's on you for that," Tim replied. "Bloody comedian."

Jester pulled out his empty pockets and smirked.

"Not a penny on me bruv! Simon will sort it. Go get 'em, champ."

Simon glared and folded his arms, quickly defused by a grin from Jester. He rolled his eyes and got up, heading for the bar, Jester in tow.

"Tim, now I have you alone, mind if I show you something?"

Harry fumbled in his pockets, hands shaking a little, producing his phone

"Christ, Harry mate. How long since you've had a proper date?"

Harry handed over the phone without answering, silence answer enough.

"Right, mate. First problem—no girl wants a knight. I mean, every girl did, but that was centuries ago." Tim paused, glancing up from the phone. "You're hiding behind this medieval stuff, aren't you? Like it's safer than just being yourself."

Even if that were true, who wouldn't rather be an ironclad knight than a suited clown?

"Try this photo," Tim continued, swiping to Harry's gallery. "This one from Christmas—Yvette put that funny hat on you, you looked a right tit. But trust me, girls will love it, plus they'll get competitive seeing my missus!"

Tim sure was a good salesman. If he could sell knackered old Fords, he could sell his knackered old brother.

"There you are. Give that a go, mate, tell me how you get on. But watch out for them scammers, will ya? Don't suppose I need to tell you that though, do I, Harold."

Harry giggled, the formal use of his name bringing him back to childhood, to digging holes in the garden and bitter but loving rivalries over Lego.

"Beer's here boys! Brothers in steel!"

They each grabbed a pint from the tray, clinked their glasses together and drank.

The night whittled away quickly, eleven threatening to turn to midnight.

"Right then, it's late. Come on, Si, let's bugger off." Jester said.

Simon offered his hand to the brothers, as Jester bounded towards the exit.

The drone of voices in the background had died down by now. Tim firmly placed his hand on Harry's shoulder, as he rose from his chair, scraping it loudly on the floor.

"Well mate, I'll see you next week. Or Sunday, if you actually bother!"

Harry and Tim smiled at one other, as he watched his brother leave.

He couldn't help but wonder what Mr Snuffles would think, if he could, of his life to date. Would he be proud?

Harry took another small swig of his pint, swirling it a little. It began to taste more bitter somehow.

Lights began to dim at the pub, the bell having rung for last orders long ago. Well, Mr Snuffles would be waiting for him. Harry watched the barmaid vigorously rubbing a rag against a spill on the bar, briefly distracted by her ponytail furiously jiggling back and forth. Imagined her husband had some fun hanging onto that thing, but quickly shook the thought from his head. Unprofessional.

Shuffled himself out of there and headed home. Wouldn't have quite so much fun gripping Mr Snuffles, but he looked forward to his hugs all the same.

Chapter 7

Harry groaned, cacophony of the phone alarm silenced, now in the kitchen. One day, the phone was going out the bloody window, but not today.

The aroma of frying egg filled his nose, soon to fill his stomach, dancing away happily at the stove.

Harry's gaze once again wandered over to his photos. This time, specifically from the medieval group's last event at Castle Rising.

Every year, they held a medieval festival, where re-enactors would come and display their crafts and hobbies—the scraping, clanging sound of steel on steel charging the atmosphere, but also the curious scents of potions and poultices from the herbalists, the stale, musty smell of tanned leather from the leatherworkers and so many more.

It wouldn't be long before this year's event, and the four of them got their own pitch to demonstrate their armours and sword-fighting techniques.

Omelette fully demolished, Harry suited and booted, ready for the office.

The fresh, briny sea air filled his lungs once more, bringing the peace and tranquillity of the ocean, the gentle caress of the autumn breeze on his walk over.

"Good morning, Harry!" Olivia began, rising from her office chair with a jump. "You have a good time at the pub last night?"

How the heck had she known about that? Clairvoyant? Secret Agent? Was she there?

"You were there?"

Olivia frowned, folding her arms across her chest.

"You didn't recognise me cleaning the bar, Harry? I would have come said hi, but my boss there is strict, and I didn't want to intrude on your gathering. I cover shifts there too, sometimes when I need the money, once or twice a month maybe."

Harry felt bile rise in his throat. The ponytail!

"So sorry, Olivia. You must have thought me rude. I'm not paying you enough, then?" Harry joked, laughing nervously.

"It's not that. I've just been saving for some armour and a sword, that's all. I saw an advert for this medieval group, it looked like fun. Have you seen it?"

Bugger.

From context it was clear—Jester had reposted the advert, and Olivia intended on joining.

Harry sighed a little, gripped his briefcase extra tight.

"Well, I'm in it actually. Maybe it's not a good idea we both belong? No offence intended, just professionalism to consider."

Harry brushed past, heading to his desk.

Olivia followed him inside, closing the door behind her as gently as possible.

"I promise, Harry, I'll be no bother, I won't intrude. It honestly just looked fun. If it doesn't feel comfortable my being there, I'll leave. That OK?"

Harry had heard her, but didn't listen. Croissants, apple turnovers, even his favourite—cinnamon swirls. All laid out in front of him, the sweet alluring scent of cinnamon and sugar calling, begging to be eaten.

"That sounds fine, Olivia, let's do that then. So these pastries...?" Harry asked expectantly.

Olivia smiled, happy little claps.

"I read something, Harry! You can put clients at ease with these. The smell of good food is calming. Oh! I got extra swirls, you said they're your favourite right?"

Had he mentioned that? Must have done, at some point.

"Besides, maybe you'll be less grumpy with a cinnamon swirl in your tummy?"

Olivia grabbed one and playfully tossed it to Harry, him fumbling fas he nearly fed it to the floor.

"Oh Olivia, I love it. I've always been too nervous to do something like this. Not the pinnacle of professionalism, office filled with pizza and pastry."

Olivia shrugged, giggling away happily to herself.

"But it is the pinnacle of pastry! Enjoy, Harry. I'll send your first client in when he's here."

Olivia skipped out the door, carefully closing it behind her.

Harry closed his eyes, savouring the gentle crunch of the swirl as the cinnamon and sugar made sweet, passionate love to his tongue. Could eat dozens of these, if his pancreas would let him.

The sharp crackle of the infernal intercom quickly broke the spell, snapping Harry back to reality.

"Sending in your next client, Harry."

Mr Raffle talked but Harry didn't listen. Just kept staring at the pastry. Finally gave in and grabbed another one, his client following suit.

"Thanks for listening, Mr Maxwell. Glad to get that off my chest."

"Absolutely. Book in again, we'll listen. Talk, I mean. Take care now."

Harry loosened his tie a little, watching him leave.

With plenty of time before his next client, he slid his hand into his pocket, producing his phone. Tapping on the app, it was time to see if Tim's adjustments had landed.

Seemed to have helped, with three interests showing.

Jennifer, 44, casual interests.

Not for Harry, but best of luck to her.

Terri, 33, chemical engineer.

That seemed interesting, and she was pretty, too. Harry stared into her deep brown eyes, juxtaposed against her bright blonde hair. That's a ponytail he could hang onto through a marriage.

> *"Hello, Terri, a pleasure. I am Harry Maxwell, scam counsellor. Psychologist, and—"*

Way too bloody formal. Wasn't a letter to His Majesty now, was it?

> *"Hi Terri, lovely to meet you. Let's have dinner? Harry."*

Still about as subtle as a rock concert, but it would have to do.

Harriet, 30, doctorate in psychology. Harry smiled warmly at her face, caring smile, deep green eyes like brilliant emeralds.

The symmetrical names did give him a smile. Easiest right swipe of his subscription. Harry leaned back in his chair, gazing off into the ceiling, imagining the psychological power duo of Harry & Harriet. Assuming she wasn't a scammer, anyway. That'd require a bit of google-fu.

Still, he wasn't ready to marry her just yet, though he was grateful to see she was likely real on the initial online search.

But Terri had responded, eager for dinner, so that would have to wait. Harry gave a little fist pump— quickly straightening his tie afterwards, slipping his phone back into his pocket. Fortunately, nobody saw that.

The door creaked open moments later, Olivia beaming a smile, carrying her signature Tupperware. She unclipped the lid with a satisfying pop, revealing an enticing, deliciously creamy macaroni cheese, cooked to perfection.

"I made your favourite, Harry! Dig in."

Truly, he wasn't paying her enough. Harry didn't need telling twice, smile quickly spreading from ear to ear. He thought back to the pizza, the swirls, the tuna sandwich—he had no rights being as skinny as he was. The swordfighting maybe?

Harry savoured every bite, the macaroni not overly soft, yet not rubbery or hard. She'd even included a layer of baked breadcrumbs on top, a true culinary sensation that cleared his mind of all woes. If he won the lottery tomorrow, he'd be hiring Olivia as his personal chef aboard his yacht.

"Think I'm going to need another gym membership if you keep feeding me like this, Olivia. Oh, your pastry idea worked a treat—pun intended! I'll give you an allowance for those from now on."

Olivia giggled.

"Ah, well, if I join the swords club, you can practise poking me with yours right here in this office, Harry!"

Harry shook his head, straightening his tie. Bile rose in his throat a little.

"Nowhere near enough room. Besides, think the clients might have a question or two if we show up here in armour, don't you?"

Olivia smiled, quickly snatching up her Tupperware and heading back out of the office. With the rest of the day free and clear, it was time for Harry to go meet with his date. It was sure to go swimmingly.

Chapter 8

Harry adjusted his tie once more, for the umpteenth time. Seems Terri was running a little late—but not by much, as Harry spotted her pushing through the door at the front of the restaurant.

Harry smiled, admiring her tight red dress. He didn't wish to stare, but needless to say Tim would be proud. Very proud.

He lifted his arm, waving her over, heart racing a mile a minute.

"Lovely to see you. I'm Harry. How was your journey here?"

Terri slumped into the chair across from him, her whole body bouncing as she did. Not particularly graceful, but definitely lingering in Harry's eye.

"Oh, just fine. Grand, even. Do have to love that Friday night traffic. Great, really."

He was no expert, but Harry did detect a slight hint of sarcasm.

"Well, I ordered an assorted platter of appetisers. Is that all right? How was work?"

Harry willed his chest to calm, heart still racing. Further than he'd got with his last date already, so that was good.

"Sure, thanks. So anyway, at work today, they made me responsible for optimising the catalytic hydrogenation process for our new benzene derivatives. The pressure differential calculations are absolutely mental—we're talking about adjusting the palladium catalyst loading by point-zero-three per cent increments to maximise yield efficiency. Of course, they expect me to recalibrate it alone! Worse still they—"

Swimmingly.

"So, look." Harry interjected. "Do you ever feel like you have trouble connecting with people? Like you've all these thoughts, these feelings, these experiences and expectations, but it's just so hard to really get that connection you long for?"

Terri contorted her face, staring at Harry.

"I have no idea what you just said to me. Why would you think I did? Are you trying to tell me you're having a bad time or something?"

Terri crossed her arms, glaring at Harry. Even more swimmingly.

"Well no, I didn't mean that. Well, I did ask you about work, so that's to be expected, right?"

He heard it before he said it, but it slipped out all the same. It might have landed if it were their third or fourth date, but his heart sank the moment his throat vibrated. Date was toast. Should have brought his swimming trunks.

Terri shuffled back out of her chair, scraping it against the floor, turning her back to Harry and heading towards the door.

Well, at least there would be appetisers.

The waiter approached, balancing a generous platter of appetisers—prawns, bruschetta, olives glistening under the bright restaurant lights.

"Your starter, sir. Will the lady be returning?"

"Stranger things have happened, but can't think of any right now. Bill, please."

The waiter offered a sympathetic nod and retreated, leaving Harry alone with enough food for two and the quiet hum of other diners' conversations.

He picked at a prawn half-heartedly. Around him, couples leaned across tables, sharing plates, smiles and laughter.

Ten minutes later, Harry pushed the barely touched platter away and sorted the bill. Time to go.

Might go get those swimming trunks, actually. Might get lucky and drown, saving him from having to tell his brother about yet another amazing, top tier date. Well, weekend ahead, and those were always peaceful. Sometimes.

Chapter 9

Breakfast sorted, Harry turned his attention to the noticeboard on his kitchen wall, gently running his finger across the smooth laminated feel of the flyer. The forge experience he gazed at wouldn't be cheap at £250 a head, but the group could certainly have an unforgettable experience together. Who didn't want to make their own medieval blades?

He decided to take it with him to see Tim and the family tomorrow, carefully pulling the pin from the board and placing the flyer on the kitchen table. Couldn't forget it there.

Harry pulled out his phone to three new texts:

"Yo Harry, want to go practise on the beach? Plastic swords bruv obvs. Jester"

Unusually straightforward for Jester, Harry thought. No quips, jests or jabs in sight. Must be under the weather, or finally employed.

"Hi Harry! It's Rachel, from the dating app. We swapped numbers a while ago, but life happened, months passed—you know. Sorry I didn't message. But I am now, if you're up for a date tomorrow? Rachel x"

Must have been over half a year since they matched and swapped numbers—it wouldn't take a bachelor's degree in psychology to know he was a plan B, ghosted and resurrected since her primary candidate didn't work out.

Still, he could use the practice. A coffee date Sunday morning was bound to go swimmingly. Might actually take the swim trunks this time.

"Coffee on the promenade, 11:30 tomorrow?
Harry x"

Another message—this time from Harriet.

"Dear Harry, I hope this message finds you well. I read your profile, and saw you counsel the victims of scams. I'm obsessed with the mind, my research often intersecting with your experience. It cannot be easy, bearing that burden, living in their grief and loss. Sorry to drone, darling. Harriet"

Harry narrowed his gaze. Harry & Harriet, both psychologists, felt a little off, as did the entire bloody essay as an introduction. Professional instincts kicking in, he looked her up online more thoroughly this time.

Dr Harriet Baker, he saw on LinkedIn. Very similar profile photo to her dating app, but more professional looking. Still digging that ponytail, though.

It would be a simple task to check she was real, too. Seemed to have an academic email. He could reach out to that—perhaps directly sharing research information.

Scammers notoriously wouldn't meet, call or video call either. All options available.

Had to wonder if he was just being paranoid. In his line of work, coincidences usually meant scams.

Fumbled through his kit bag for his plastic sword, heavy in his hand, then popped his phone out for a moment and called Jester.

"Harry! My guy! You coming out then? Let's get you some training in, maybe help you suck a bit less for the event at Castle Rising, bruv? Come on, I'll even let you buy me another ice cream."

Dashed that employment theory, then.

"I'd like that. Thanks, Jester. I'll see you there in ten. To save you the theatrics, yes, I'll get us both ice cream first."

Jester chuckled down the phone.

"Safe! See you soon, bruv."

With a click, the call was over. Back into the pocket with the phone, and out the door with Harry.

The brisk walk to the promenade was cool and crisp, gulls cawing overhead, sea air filling his spirits. Harry felt a few wandering gazes, possibly from the plastic sword he held. They must have lacked whimsy or imagination.

"Pay the lady, Harry! Here you go."

Jester had got a jump on the ice creams—well, ordering them, but certainly not remuneration.

Harry gratefully accepted the cone, gleefully feeling the smooth, strawberry tones against his tongue.

"Jester, you never pay for anything, much less pay attention. How'd you know I like strawberry?"

Jester gestured over to the nearby bench. "Oh, she told me. Hasn't shut up about you since she arrived, bruv."

Olivia was sitting on a nearby bench, holding Jester's plastic swords. Seemed she'd got a jump on the medieval group, opting to meet with Jester first.

"Hi Harry!" she began, skipping over, gleeful smile plastered on her face—along with copious quantities of strawberry lipstick. "I asked the group leader to come get some training before next Thursday. It's good to see you here, too."

She came over and hugged Harry tightly. It felt rude for him to challenge that in front of Jester, but he responded by gently patting her on the head.

"Right, well, good to see you too, Olivia. Well then, let's train some, shall— Hold on a moment. Group leader?"

Jester grinned wide, shrugging his shoulders, starting to giggle.

"I started this thing! Well, Simon too. Still, Jester rules bruv."

Harry gripped his hilt tightly, narrowing his gaze.

"And how does Simon feel about that?"

Jester's glee popped like a cheap party balloon.

"Fine, whatever. You got me. I don't want no beef with the big man. Democracy it is. Well, come on, let's get to fighting then!"

Jester grabbed his two plastic swords, spinning them with precision, feet gently shuffling the sand away beneath his trainers.

Olivia folded her arms, back on the bench, staring intently at Harry as he moved in, circling around Jester.

"Tim is faster than you, bruv—accept it. But you're taller, stronger. You can beat him the same way Simon beats me, but you've got to practise. Maybe we should swap that sword of yours out for something longer, too?"

Harry circled around Jester, considering.

"I could see Harry with a longsword myself. Maybe even a claymore? That would look good, Harry!" Olivia chimed in from her perch on the bench.

Jester stopped circling and leaned in close to Harry.

"Yo, I like her, Harry. Does her research. She's right, you know, she knows her stuff. You hitting that or what?"

Harry's gripped the warm plastic hilt in his palm extra hard.

"Of course not! Now, are we practising or not?"

Jester sprang back into action, dancing through the sand, displacing it as he shuffled. He spun his swords, arcing and relentless sweeps towards Harry.

Harry gripped the hilt firmly, moving to intercept each blow, the shocks vibrating through his wrist. He attempted a counterattack, aiming for Jester's head.

Jester ducked out of the way, sword raised. "Yo! No head blows with the plastic, unless helmed."

Harry's sword raised simultaneously, signalling a break in combat. "Bugger, sorry Jester. I won't forget again. Lots on my mind."

The fighting continued for a little while, until the next break was agreed, swords raised. Olivia rushed to her feet.

"Right then, missy. Your turn?" Jester said, offering the hilt of a plastic sword to Olivia.

"Not today, sorry. Think I'll go see the penguin exhibit. You coming, Harry?" Olivia asked expectantly.

"Best stay here and train more. Enjoy the exhibit, Olivia. See you Monday."

Olivia shrugged and skipped off happily towards her penguins.

Jester beckoned for Harry to follow to the nearby metal bench with a brief twist of his neck.

"Harry, bruv. Are you blind, or just stupid?"

Extra sharp, coming from this clown.

"Olly is obviously into you, mate. I look at a Big Mac the way she looks at you. You gonna get it or what? Trust me, I already tried my luck. Flat-out refused, cold as the sea, man. But you show up? Different girl, innit."

Harry sighed, staring down at an errant piece of chewed gum on the floor.

"We're colleagues, and I'm old enough to be her dad. Not on the cards. It's been briefly touched on, and there's a mutual respect of boundaries now."

Jester pointed at Harry, laughing maniacally.

"Bloody hell bruv! You actually believe that, don't you? Scamming yourself there, Harry. Whatever, let's go train some more."

Jester sprang to his feet, taunting Harry to come fight once more with his finger. Harry sighed, gripped his sword tightly, and followed.

The waves crashed against the shore, as the thunk of plastic swords crashed against one another. Harry looked over at the sea, opening his arm to a strike from Jester.

The pain was very brief, just a short snap and nothing more.

"Head in the bloody game, man. What, you too busy thinking about Olly in a nightie?"

There were times Harry truly wished to wallop Jester for real, but only briefly. He smiled, raising his sword for the training to end.

"Thanks, Jester. I'd like to beat Tim some day."

Jester put his arm round Harry.

"Good short-term goal, my man, and you can do it. But think big. Get on my level, on Simon's. You keep training, bruv, you can do it. I see greatness in both you boys. Do the work."

The irony wasn't lost on Harry, trying his best not to grin.

"I'm off home, man. But another ice cream before we go wouldn't hurt, would it?"

"Fine, but Jester, one day you'll be buying me an ice cream. When you're back on your feet. Deal?"

Harry reached out his hand, Jester gladly grabbing it with both.

"Deal! Harry, you a legend!"

Two sugary, sweet treats later and the boys parted ways, Harry off home. Big day tomorrow, best get the swimming trunks ready.

Chapter 10

Harry shook his head, pushed himself up against the soft cotton sheet and stood, still groggy from a night of back and forth texting with Harriet. The coffee date with Rachel wouldn't be long, but try telling that to the butterflies.

Harry carefully and methodically scraped his razor against his skin, feeling it scratch as he shaved. He rubbed some slimy, sticky hair gel through his fringe, trying to style it, ready for a morning stroll along the promenade.

One pleasant stroll later, brine in his lungs, Harry placed his hand against the cold wooden door, pushing it open and entering the coffee shop. The dull drone of patrons at tables prodded at his ears.

Harry smiled as he spotted a corner table with a gorgeous view of the sea. Perfect.

He was five minutes early, but that didn't matter. He could grab a harsh, stimulating shot of espresso before Rachel arrived.

Phone produced from his pocket, tapping on the coffee shop app. A couple of minutes passed, the waitress dropping it by with a cheery smile.

Harry's face contorted as the bitter espresso startled his taste buds, gripping the wood of the table hard. Still, that would wake him up in time for the date.

Harry fumbled for his phone and checked the time—she was ten minutes late. Looked for a tie to tighten, found none.

Ten more minutes passed by, Harry deciding to check his phone again. He slid his finger across the screen, tapping on his messages. He went to text Rachel only to see his number had been blocked.

Harry chuckled, then slumped in his chair. Shortest date yet. Definitely time to renew that pool membership, go for a swim.

"Will you be ordering another drink, sir?" the waitress asked, gently probing Harry.

"Why, you joining me?"

She offered a sympathetic smile and shook her head. Figures.

Off to the promenade, Harry hunted down his favourite bench. Harry sighed, seeing it already occupied. He opted to keep walking, taking in the sea air, one salty lungful at a time.

Rachel had likely made up with her prime candidate. Couldn't be bothered to explain that, so just blocked Harry. Either that or she saw his Facebook photo, face messier than a hoarder's flat. Phone vibrated with a call from his brother.

"Harry mate, you still coming for roast then? Yvette's making toad in the hole, special for you. Boys are mental about seeing Uncle Harry. Aren't you, boys?"

Harry winced, briefly pulling his phone away from his ear as the boys screeched in excitement.

"Bloody hell mate, I dunno if you heard that, but they're rabid. Come on down when you want, yeah? Dinner at three."

Definitely heard it. Probably heard it in China.

His phone buzzed with a text from Harriet.

*"Good morning, Harry. I hope your coffee date
goes wonderfully. You deserve genuine connection
with someone who appreciates your depth.
Looking forward to continuing our discussion
later, darling. Almost hoping your little coffee date
goes nowhere. Harriet x"*

Thoughtful.

Harry headed home to collect the blacksmithing flyer, remembering he'd strategically placed Mr Snuffles on top of it so he wouldn't forget. Great guy, that bunny, ever helpful, ever loyal. Smashing listener, too.

The drive to Tim's bungalow felt lighter despite the morning's disappointment. Tree-lined roads stretched ahead, autumn leaves rustling in the breeze.

Pulling up in the driveway, he could barely open his car door before the front door of the house burst open, two small bodies hurtling towards him.

"Uncle Harry! Uncle Harry!"

Steve and Tom collided with his legs simultaneously, Harry smiling wide.

"All right, boys, let your bloody uncle breathe!" Tim appeared, wrestling the children back. "Come in, mate, Yvette's got the kettle on."

The house smelt of baking batter and sausages, warmth radiating from both the kitchen and his family's welcome. Yvette appeared, flour dusting her apron and a wooden spoon in hand, smiling warmly at Harry.

"Harry! How lovely. Boys, go wash your hands, dinner's nearly ready."

"Uncle Harry, why don't you have a wife?" Steve blurted out, ignoring Mum completely.

"Steve!" Yvette scolded, but Harry held up his hand.

"That's all right. Good question, Steve. I'm trying to find one right now, kiddo. But these things take time."

"But you're old," Tom added helpfully. "Daddy says you're a dinosaur."

Tim appeared behind his sons, grinning sheepishly. "Cheers for that, Tom."

Harry laughed despite himself. "Well, Daddy's got a point. But I'm working on it. I'll have my own little rugrats one day, boys, count on it."

Harry dropped his fork, metal clanging against the table as the skewered potato patiently waited in the gravy. He fumbled in his pocket, looking for the blacksmithing experience flyer, having almost forgotten. He had to carefully evade, pulling his arm away, before grubby little mitts snatched it from him.

"Wow! Is that sword-making? Can we come, Uncle Harry? Please? We'll be good! Please!" Steve pleaded.

"It's for adults only. Sorry, kiddo," Harry explained. "But Tim, they're surely old enough to come watch us at swords sometime instead?"

Tim narrowed his gaze, gently stamping Harry's foot, ever so slightly shaking his head. Ah, kid-free time, was it. That made sense.

Tim took the flyer and examined it whilst carefully cutting his son's sausage. "Two-fifty each? Bit steep, mate. Worth it though—the lads would love making proper blades. But there's no way Jester's affording this, is there?"

"What about safety?" Yvette interjected practically. "Four grown men with hammers and molten metal? Though, the thought of Tim shirtless and hammering an anvil—meow!"

Harry smiled, watching them laugh together—quickly followed by the twin cacophony of "Ewww! Mum!"

Harry took back the flyer. "Don't worry, there's a master blacksmith watching over us, he owns the forge. Grizzled veteran."

"Sounds great, mate!" Tim decided. "When?"

"Perhaps before our big day at Castle Rising? See what the brothers think?"

Dinner complete and back in the lounge, Harry watched Tim rough-housing with the boys, their laughter filling the room. His phone buzzed—another message from Harriet.

> *"I hope your family time is relaxing, Harry! I've been researching victim recovery methodologies and found your published paper on shame cycles in fraud victims. Eye-opening, truly. Your insights into the psychology of financial manipulation are mesmerising. I'd love to discuss this with you more, darling. Harriet x"*

Harry blinked at the screen. She'd found his academic work? A flag of some kind, but what colour he couldn't be sure. Red and green? Brown? Brown.

Harry got up and pulled on his coat.

"Cheers for having me, Tim. Meant a lot."

"You're family, you muppet. Always welcome here. Boys and Yvette agree. Don't worry so much about dating, mate. You've got this."

The drive home carried warmth that lasted until Harry pulled into his empty driveway. His phone showed another message from Harriet.

> *"Your research on trust rebuilding after betrayal is fascinating, Harry. I find myself wondering how you maintain such empathy after witnessing so much human cruelty. You must be so kind and caring. Sleep well. Harriet x"*

Harry smiled as he climbed into bed, Mr Snuffles now resuming his vigil. Perhaps intellectual connection was a form of intimacy too, though Harry did have to wonder why she seemed so keen.

Chapter 11

"Olivia, lovely to see you. You seem happy today. Good weekend?" Harry asked, stepping into the office lobby.

Olivia clapped happily, almost bouncing on the spot.

"Yep! I got my armour, and my sword too! Want to see?"

Harry raised an eyebrow. "Surely you don't have them here?"

Olivia frowned and folded her arms across her chest. "It's not like I'm going to use them, Harry. Come on, it's fine."

Harry sighed and shook his head. "I don't think my personal liability insurance will cover it, Olivia. Are you able to get them home?"

Olivia put her hands behind her back again, staring at the ceiling.

"Not really. Monday is our busy day. But you can take me at lunch?"

Harry felt a tightness in his chest, wrestling with his tie.

"Yeah, that'll work. We may miss lunch though."

Olivia grinned wide and shrugged her shoulders, before gesturing to his office. "No we won't!"

Harry's eyes opened wide, as if seeing a beautiful mirage of flavour, all manner of sandwiches before him. The smell most overpowering of them all was coffee, which practically magnetised his throat towards it.

Harry pondered for a moment, then smiled warmly back at Olivia.

"This is really thoughtful, Olivia. Our busy day, so you've outdone yourself—the clients will be so pleased."

He tugged at his tie before continuing.

"I'll make sure to reimburse you for the coffee maker. Never did take the plunge myself, but I always meant to—I'm glad you've given me that push."

Olivia bounced on the spot a little, before responding.

"Speaking of which, you've got a busy day. More whiskey barrel scams I'm afraid. Oh, and that scammer guy is back."

Harry scratched his chin, narrowing his gaze. "Scammer guy? Oh, you mean Sareth."

Olivia nodded, walking out of the room, blowing Harry a kiss as she pulled the door shut.

Harry rolled his eyes, grabbing a cinnamon swirl and taking a swig of freshly brewed coffee, letting it linger.

Harry felt his phone getting heavier and heavier in his pocket as he waited patiently for his first client, clock ticking away in his gaze, one second at a time.

Well, just one little peek. Might have won the lottery last night, though probably had more chance of nailing a date.

Text message from Harriet:

"I'm sure you're going to be busy today, darling. Do your thing, be you, be brilliant. I own your first book now, by the way—you'll have to sign it for me some time. Harriet x"

She really was keen. Academic interest? Personal interest? Sydney Opera House for sale?

Harry was startled shortly by his office door creaking open, Sareth pushing his way inside.

"Uh, hi Harry. I can sit?"

Harry nodded, gesturing.

Sareth carefully sat on the edge of the middle seat, purposefully ignoring the feast before him.

"Sareth, good to see you again," Harry said, brushing any remaining crumbs of a cinnamon swirl from his lap.

"Thank you. So, well, I've been trying to keep busy here. Soon, I can work. How I should have done all along. They say they are going to put me into an informational technology course, just as I was told before in Phnom Penh. It didn't feel nice, Mr Harry."

Sareth scraped his feet across the carpet a little, glaring at an apple turnover.

"Sareth, help yourself if you want a pastry, or a sandwich. Look, that's understandable. That's exactly the ruse they told you in the first place—IT job in England, sign up and pay us, off you go. You weren't to know what was coming."

Sareth lowered his head, glaring at the floor.

"It all came back. The whipping. The scamming. It was a prison. Others, still trapped. They can't leave and I can't help."

Sareth rubbed a finger against his eye, head still hung low.

"But you survived. You claimed asylum in the United Kingdom, and you told us your tale. Other places like the compound you were enslaved in have been shut down, prisoners freed."

Harry paused a beat, tapping his fingers on the desk a little, before continuing.

"Yes, you scammed people there, and you have to come to terms with that—but can you honestly sit there and say you had any other choice? They whipped you literally, Sareth. Don't let them whip you figuratively, too."

Sareth looked over at Harry, quizzical expression.

"Like... They whip my mind now, Mr Harry?"

"Right, but only if you let them."

A few moments passed, Sareth's attention now turned to a tuna sandwich. Harry smiled, gesturing his arm towards it, Sareth reluctantly accepting.

Harry joined him, devouring another crusty, sugary cinnamon swirl. The gym membership now felt like an inevitability.

"Well... I can maybe help people, in this job. If I pass the training? And then I'm good, I'm helping."

"You can never unscam your victims, but you get to decide every day if you want to be a good person or not. You're already good in my eyes, Sareth. You came here and asked for help—you are clearly struggling over both what you did and why you did it. Good people consider consequences."

Sareth managed to curl up a little smile.

"Thank you, Mr Harry. Can I take a cinnamon wheel too? You look at this like I look at my girlfriend, yes?"

Harry and Sareth chuckled together. Time to look up that gym number, probably.

"Oh, I'm simply addicted. I'll need to buy a gym soon, if I keep this up. Well, let me know how that course goes, Sareth. My secretary likes to study new IT things too, ask her. See you soon."

Sareth managed a little wave, winking at Harry as he grabbed a cinnamon swirl, shuffling meekly back out the door.

Olivia pushed through the door, kit bag overpowering her meagre muscles. Harry rushed up from his chair, almost dropping it onto the carpet, and sprang over to help.

His hand met Olivia's on the strap, which he quickly moved away.

"Sorry, Olivia. Right, let's get this in the car then?"

Standing next to her, the strawberry fragrance she wore mingled happily with his nostrils, as the strawberry colour filled Olivia's cheeks.

"Mmhmm. Off to mine then!"

Harry hauled her kit bag onto his shoulder, the weight pulling against him.

"Ah, Olivia. My keys please, left breast pocket."

Harry looked away as Olivia slid a hand onto his side, and one into his breast pocket, fumbling for the keys.

"Got it!" she announced proudly, dangling the keys in front of Harry, a hand still lingering on his side, nerves fraying in his chest. He gestured with his neck towards the boot, where he plonked the heavy kit bag.

"Hop in, let's sort this. Can't be late for my next whiskey barrel scam. Oh, speaking of which, Olivia?"

She turned to Harry, eyes widened, grinning.

"Do try not to schedule those back to back in future?"

They both started to chuckle as they climbed in, strapped up and set off.

Chapter 12

They pulled up to the block of flats where Olivia lived. The building seemed ancient, cracks in the bricks, the weather wearing and denting them. A roof tile hung loose, desperately clinging on for dear life. Harry wondered how long it had been struggling there against the elements.

He sighed, gripping the steering wheel.

"All right, go pop your kit in, Olivia. Lunch is fast evaporating."

Olivia hopped out and opened the boot.

"It's a bit heavy, Harry. Can I have a hand?"

His grip strangled the leather of the wheel, creaking beneath his hands.

"How on earth did you get that to the office in the first place? You may need two separate kit bags, Olivia, you need to be able to carry them."

Harry climbed out the car and hoisted the kit bag over his shoulder.

"Oh, I had it delivered there! I'm sorry, I just really wanted you to see it. I wasn't thinking."

Olivia beckoned Harry to follow with her finger, eyes fixed on him as he lugged the heavy bag.

She jammed the key into her ground-floor flat, shoving the door open hard. It resisted, showing signs of wear.

Harry pushed past her, hastily dropping the heavy kit bag on the sofa.

Pinks, purples, reds everywhere. A vast contrast to the familiar feel of magnolia and grey.

Harry narrowed his gaze. Photographs adorned the walls—Olivia smiling at her work desk, grinning right at the camera. Red pandas, behind glass. Penguins waddling across ice. Olivia once more, certificate of some kind. One of himself, adjusting his tie, cheap blue suit and even cheaper smile. Taken from outside his office window? Peculiar angle.

"When did you take this one?" Harry asked.

"Ages ago! You looked so professional. Couldn't help myself!"

Harry grabbed his tie, loosening it as it gripped at his throat.

"Do you like the penguin photo, Harry? It's from that exhibit I told you about," Olivia beamed with a smile.

"Yep. Off we pop then."

"Oh wait, Harry! You haven't seen the armour properly yet. I could try some of it on for you? Come give me a hand?" Olivia's eyes brightened.

Didn't have time to play dress-up. Office to run.

"I'm sure it's lovely, Olivia, but we really need to get back. I've another client soon. Bring it on Thursday to swords, we'll sort it then."

"Of course! Thursday it is then. I'm just so excited to show you!"

As Harry waited by the door, his gaze wandered across her small bookshelf. Among romance novels and self-help books, he spotted a familiar spine.

"Ah, my first book. A first edition, too," he said, nodding towards *'Introduction to Cybercrime.'*

She followed his gaze, brightening immediately.

"Yes! I bought it after I started working for you, remember? I love it. Would you sign it for me sometime?"

"Of course, bring it to the office. Or I could give you another copy—you can hand this one to a friend."

"I'd love that," she said, already moving towards the door, smile faltering once more. "Shall we head back then, Harry?"

Harry walked briskly towards his car, away from the overbearing colours of the flat, hopping in and belting up.

Harry gripped the wheel a little tighter, creaking the leather beneath his hands.

He almost wanted to ask about the absence of family photos. The lack of them nagged at his mind, a little woodpecker on the side of his head drilling away. Boundaries blurred a little today.

"You looked very tense on the drive back, Harry. Are you all right?" Olivia suggested gently, placing a hand meekly on his shoulder.

"I'm fine, Olivia. Just something on my mind." Harry paused, his professional instincts overriding his discomfort. "I couldn't help but notice—there were no family photos in your flat. I hope you don't mind me asking, but why is that?"

Olivia's hand slipped from his shoulder. She stared down at her lap.

"Oh. That." Her voice became smaller, quieter. "I was in foster care, actually. From when I was little until eighteen. Never really had a proper family to photograph, I suppose."

Bugger.

"I'm sorry, Olivia. That must have been difficult. I've lost so much in my life, but you never had it to lose."

Olivia smiled, patting Harry on the shoulder.

"It was lonely. Moving house often, never really fitting in." She looked up at him, eyes glistening slightly.

"Foster families were nice, but you always knew you were temporary. I felt like a guest, not a daughter. I never really had a proper home."

Harry nodded gently.

"I suppose you likely find it hard making friends your age, too?"

Olivia frowned.

"I just don't seem to have much in common with people my age. They want to go clubbing and get high, I want to learn new things. I'm always looking at technology, science, psychology, and of course animals!"

Like those cute waddling penguins.

"Well, don't isolate yourself, Olivia. You've a lot to give the world. Maybe a husband some day, too. Or a wife, whatever floats your boat."

Harry chuckled, earning a roll of Olivia's eyes.

"I just hope he's even half the man you are, Harry Maxwell."

Olivia's eyes twinkled as she gazed at Harry.

"Right, well. Let's get back to it then."

Stepping into the office once more, Olivia back at her desk, Harry asked "Right then. What's next for the afternoon?"

"Whiskey barrel scam. Sorry."

Great. He might need to buy some himself if this kept up.

The rest of the day passed in a blur, the thought of seeing another bottle of whiskey daring bile to rise from Harry's stomach.

He left Olivia tapping away at her keyboard, and strolled out to the promenade, hunting for his favourite metal friend.

There it sat, free as a bird, waiting for him to feel the cold snap as he sat on it, breathing deeply the salty sea air once more.

The waves calmly washed against the shore, washing the bitter stench of whiskey from his nose.

Harry shuddered, then reached into his pocket, fumbling for his phone.

> *"Hello, brothers in steel, I showed Tim this flyer yesterday. Thoughts?"*

Harry dug into his pockets, straightening out the bent flyer, carefully snapping a photo of it. His finger hovered over send for a moment.

Harry was startled as someone tousled his hair from behind, phone flying through the air. Thankfully, the nimble nitwit behind him caught it, dexterous as ever.

"Harry, bruv! What you got here? Oh nice one, that looks wicked. I'm a bit poor though, innit."

Jester carelessly tossed his phone back towards him.

Harry fumbled, heart racing, but caught it just about. Back in the pocket.

"Jester, good to see you. How'd you know I was here?"

Jester chuckled, slapping himself on the knee.

"Come on, man, you're twice as predictable as the bloody sunrise! Where else were you gonna be? I can read you like a book, bruv—only book of yours I'm ever gonna read, by the way."

Jester flopped himself onto the bench, Harry straightening his tie, resisting the urge to shuffle away.

"I already spoke to the cooler brother, and the big man, about this forge thing, bruv. Simon's gonna spot me two hundred, I just gotta find the rest. It's doable, mate, very doable. Get us in, we'll have a laugh."

Jester patted Harry on the back.

"You may struggle to pay him back without a job," Harry bluntly stated.

Jester glared at his feet.

"Working on it, working on it, mate. Why don't you just fire that weirdo and I'll be your front office guy, your main man? Jester 'n' Harry, now that's a sitcom I'd watch!"

Harry looked Jester right in the eye, chuckling heavily.

Jester grinned, taking it in stride.

"All right, all right. Maybe not then, bruv. Right well, get us an ice cream will ya, Harry?"

Harry rolled his eyes, frowned, and reached into his pocket, feeling the worn leather of his wallet. At least Jester hadn't asked him to buy a shot of bloody whiskey.

Chapter 13

Harry lay in bed, cosy and warm, Mr Snuffles nearby staring away with his button eyes. Buzz.

> *"Harry darling, did you have a good day at work? I was reading your review about the woefully inadequate support systems in place for scam victims. Nail on the head, dear. Still, I think it may be time for us to have a little call, don't you? I'm prepared now. Harriet x"*

Right. Wasn't going to get invested without some kind of reassurance.

> *"Good idea. Why not let me send my research directly to your academic email? You can use it to inform your own."*

This was the part where she would say no, find an excuse, and he'd have wasted his time on a sodding scammer.

Seconds stretched into minutes, Harry gnawing away at his nails.

> *"That would be lovely, darling. Feel free to email me there, no problem."*

No way in hell a scammer would agree to that.

Reassured, Harry hugged his bunny goodnight, and closed his eyes, drifting off to sleep.

Several hours later, the horrendous, dreadful cacophony of "Barbie Girl" once again launched a relentless assault on his eardrums. Shot up, shower, shave, suit, set.

He didn't bother with the eggs today. Seemed pointless, Olivia most likely bringing the feast he was quickly growing accustomed to. Off he went, briny sea air hitting his lungs once more as he headed to the office.

"Morning, Harry!" Olivia beamed, in before Harry, bright and early as always.

First in, last out, as ever.

Harry nodded as he strolled past Olivia, her gaze fixed on him the entire distance.

Harry was greeted by the now familiar smells of bitter, stimulating coffee mingling happily with sugary sweetness. Without hesitation, he popped a cinnamon swirl in his mouth, crunching down on the delicious flaky pastry.

A buzz from the intercom jolted Harry, breaking the spell.

"Juliet Patrick is here to see you. Sending her in."

Harry wiped the crumbs of pastry from his mouth, straightening his tie. He rose to his feet, beckoning her over.

Her energy was fierce, her appeal extraordinary. She had fiery ginger hair with freckles symmetrically dotted about her face. Intense, deep green eyes sparkling like emeralds. When she entered a room, people noticed, no doubt. He sure did.

She sat in the corner of the sofa, legs folded, arms across her chest.

"Hi there, nice to meet you. I'm Harry Maxwell, Harry's fine. Pastry, sandwich? Bottle of water?"

She didn't look at him, simply hunched up further into her little folded shell.

Harry leaned in a little closer, lowering his voice an octave or two.

"I tell you what. I'll eat one of these cinnamon swirls in front of you, that way you won't feel so guilty having one. I mean, it's my second already and you're my first client, so if anything maybe I should be the one with the guilt."

A brief smirk emerged from his client, slightly loosening her shoulders, now daring to gaze at the assortment before her. She grabbed a chocolate Danish.

"Juliet. Jules, to friends."

Her voice was barely a whisper, carrying a world of pain and sorrow behind each broken word. She nibbled gently on the Danish.

"Well Jules, I'm here to listen, to help—to care. I've read your form. I'm really sorry. You're safe in here. Tell me, what happened?"

Jules closed her eyes, an errant tear escaping.

"I... I finally found him. I found my Romeo."

Harry smirked a little. Romeo and Juliet. Almost as delicious as the pastry.

"I finally found my man after all this time. I'm twenty-eight now, my sister's already married and pregnant at twenty-five! Things were finally going my way. Not fair."

Jules began to cry more openly, quickly brushing the tears away and stopping herself.

"So... You met him on a dating app, and you hit it off. What went wrong?"

"He made me feel so special. I get told I'm pretty all the time, it's just words. But Javier, my Romeo, he made me feel beautiful. He told me he'd never met someone like me before, never loved someone like me before—it was a whirlwind. He swept me off my feet."

Jules clawed at the sofa, glaring through Harry.

"Swept me off my feet as he pulled the wool over my eyes, and the money out of my purse. I had nothing left to give him, and he's just gone. Number disconnected, profile deleted, dreams shattered into dust."

She slumped back in her chair, now glaring at the apple turnovers, taunting her from the table.

"Best part, I'm... I'm supposed to host my sister's baby shower next week. I can't bring myself to tell her what happened. She just won't understand!"

Harry drifted off momentarily, looking through her blazing emerald eyes, beyond to his brother.

"She's family, Jules. Show her your heart. She won't be another Javier. Turn to her in your time of need and she'll be there. Her family is your family, the love you share is fierce as flame."

Jules scraped her feet across the carpet, standing. She grabbed a tuna sandwich, tearing it to shreds, nearly swallowing it whole.

After a brief but captivating display, she grinned at Harry.

"So sorry. I haven't really eaten properly since this all started. I'm glad you have these. You're sweet, Harry."

Harry grinned back. "Can't take the credit for these I'm afraid. Olivia out front sorts this all out."

Jules' eyes widened.

"That cow? Stared daggers at me the moment I got here, I swear. She not used to seeing pretty girls or something?"

Harry raised an eyebrow.

"Ah, I'm sorry you feel that way. I can assure you, we're all professionals here. She was probably just lost in thought."

Harry sighed, tapping his fingers against the desk.

"Still, I'm not dismissing what you've said—your feelings matter. You're clearly uncomfortable, so I'll talk with her. Thank you for bringing that to my attention."

Jules nodded, grabbing a cheese sandwich and stuffing it into her pocket, as she opened the door.

"Say Harry? You're really sweet, and I don't see a ring on your finger. Fancy a date?"

Quick flash of Jules with a ponytail snapped into his head, shaking it quickly away.

"Um, I'm so sorry, Jules. I mustn't date clients."

She shrugged, pulling the door fully open.

"Your loss! See you next time, Harry."

She blew him a kiss, and grinned wide, pulling a face towards Olivia as she strutted out of the office.

Lunchtime.

Olivia shuffled through the door, closing it softly behind her, smiling warmly at Harry.

"Harry, can I ask you something?" she began, before he'd had a chance to jump in.

He nodded.

"Why exactly are there so many whiskey barrel scams?"

"Ah! Well, they're seasonal, Olivia. They change with the times, exactly like sales—notice the cola-drinking bear at Christmas time? Scams and sales are the exact same skill set! It's just the ending that's... different."

Harry coughed then adjusted his tie..

"Olivia, my first client today felt unwelcomed, that you may have been glaring. I understand victim psychology may have projected that onto you—beautiful women often have subconscious competitive elements between them—but I thought I'd best bring it to your attention."

Bugger, that definitely came out wrong.

"Oh! Thank you, Harry. Sweetheart, aren't you. Um, I was just concerned about her, Harry, that's all. She seemed a little off, something just didn't sit right with me. Maybe she was feeling fragile."

"I'm sure of your professionalism, you needn't worry about that. We just need to be aware some clients are extra fragile, in a business like this."

Olivia sat on the sofa, arms across her chest.

"Did I hear her ask you on a date, Harry? That's so inappropriate, isn't it! I'm just glad I heard you decline it—ethical, good man that you are. Oh, I wasn't eavesdropping, by the way—she'd held the door open. Theatrics, maybe?"

Harry smirked, grabbing a cheese sandwich.

"Seems so. Well, let's have some lunch, it'll soon be time for more tales of whiskey and woe. Until the next big scam, whatever that may be."

"I think retro games consoles myself. From what I've seen online, they're really making money now. Something to keep our eye on."

Easy, casual conversation quickly whittled away the lunchtime minutes, before another session with Sareth and his redemption and recovery from the Cambodian scam compound rounded off the day. He'd resolved to write a book himself, try to open people's eyes.

With home time fast approaching, Harry drafted an email to Harriet's academic inbox.

"Dear Dr Baker,

Please find enclosed my research on shame cycles in financial fraud and provable insufficiency in support services.

Hope this research finds you well,

Fondest regards,

Harry Maxwell"

With that fired off, he powered down his computer, and rose to his feet. A buzz from his phone distracted him. He slipped his hand into the silky fabric, producing his phone.

> *"Lads, forge experience is on! Friday night, be there or be... Well, just be there. Harold mate, you're buying the drinks down the pub tonight. We'll talk finances there. Brothers in steel!"*

Harry smiled, slipping his phone back into his pocket. Off he went to see Tim and the boys, leaving Olivia to her station once more. Still, knot in his stomach having sent that academic email. Now, it was a waiting game.

Chapter 14

Harry rushed home, eager to pull off the choking tie and constricting suit, weary of it wrapping him in a fabric cage. His phone buzzed in his pocket.

> *"Harry darling, got your email. Thank you. I've run some statistical analyses on your data, and come to the same conclusions! I'm responding here as University monitors my communications, darling. I've attached my own results from my personal. Harriet x"*

Fired up his laptop, checked her results. Seemed informed, intelligent, nearly perfect. So why the beaver, gnawing at his thoughts? Too many scam victims, too much caution?

He set foot outside, grateful to have traded his awful loafers for some worn, soft, bouncy trainers.

Made his way to the pub, joining his brothers.

"Harry, bruv! Over here!"

Jester's booming voice echoed in Harry's ears, several octaves above the incessant drone of pub patrons nagging away at his senses.

The air smelt of stale beer and sweat as he wandered over to join the boys, already gathered round.

Harry carefully looked around, narrowing his gaze, specifically looking for signs of Olivia. None to be found, easing the tightness in his chest.

Trip to the bar, bringing a tray with four pints and plonking it on the table, Harry picked up his one and turned his gaze to Tim, unseasonably quiet.

"Timothy? You all right?"

Tim downed his beer, chugging hard, belching.

"I will be after another one or two of these things, Harold! Fetch!"

Harry sighed, relenting, dragging himself to the bar for more beers.

"Right. I've got everyone another one. I'm not getting up again for a while," Harry announced.

"You haven't been on any dates since last week? Come on, where's that double date I keep promising Yvette?" Tim prodded.

Jester put his arms around both brothers.

"Listen, boys, just get Harry married to that sexy secretary of his. She's well up for Harry, Tim mate, you should see how she looks at him. Like Simon looking at fish and chips."

Simon grunted, eyes opening wide at the thought of freshly fried fish and chips cooked in beef dripping.

"Oh yeah? Well, what's all this then, Harold?" Tim probed, perking up.

Harry frowned, glaring daggers at Jester, shrugging his hand from his shoulder.

"Nothing like that. She's my employee, and that's that. I'm friendly with her, certainly, but it isn't like—it isn't like that. I'm a professional."

Jester began laughing, pointing at Harry.

"*I'm a professional!* Bollocks mate! Just fire her, marry her, and bring us on board, bruv. Win, win, win."

Harry sighed deeply, trying to filter out the incessant droning of the patrons around.

"Give it a rest, Jester mate. Harry's said his piece. Leave him be." Tim said, as he drained half his next pint, slamming the glass against the table—thud echoing in Harry's ears.

The walls of the pub seemed to draw slightly inward, voices echoing through Harry's head, the infernal droning. He scraped his chair back against the laminate floor and walked outside to the beer garden, glass in hand.

The briny air filled his lungs once more, the incessant chatter feeling more like a distant hum from outside. The crisp, bitter chill of the autumn air was a welcome contrast to the heat and noise of the crowd inside.

The others quickly joined Harry outside, and led him to a corner table.

"Good idea, Harold mate. Getting a bit tense in there. Right, boys. The brothers in steel here got a trip planned. Top bloke that he is, Simon's covering Jester. You all right for yours, Harry?"

Harry slipped his hand into his pocket, checking his banking app. He tapped on it and sighed.

"Yeah I am, but I've got to be careful. I'm waiting on some refunds—really should chase those. Yourself, Tim?"

Tim grinned from ear to ear, raising a glass.

"I'm grand, mate. Best week's sales I've had all year. I'll cover the four of us, if need be. Just let me know."

"I'm really looking forward to this bruv. What do we even forge? Daggers or something?" Jester asked.

"Claymore!" roared Simon, garnering the attention of the handful of other patrons in the beer garden.

The four of them giggled together in unison, Harry's head feeling a little lighter.

They whittled away the hours, sipping pints, before Jester and Simon headed off.

"Harold—let's have us a chat."

Harry narrowed his gaze, heart starting to beat faster.

"I've been offered my own dealership, mate. It's in bloody Newcastle, though. More money, more stress, but might as well be in Nigeria for how far away I'd be."

Tim's shift in his usual spirits made sense now. He was at a crossroads, a defining moment, and looking to his brother for guidance.

"You do what's right for you and your family, Tim. We'll all be fine here, by the coast, if you do decide to go. Not to say you won't be missed—but we'll still have video calls and the like."

Harry's mind flicked back to Harriet, briefly, before focusing on his brother.

"Mate, that's just it. I don't think I want it. The extra stress, moving away—I sell cars, mate. I'm bloody good at it. But management doesn't feel like my thing—you know?"

Harry gazed off into the distance, pensive. He did know, in his own way.

"Then don't take it, Tim, and keep being great at what you do. Great, and happy. Being happy is what it's all about isn't it? You taught me that."

Tim grabbed Harry's shoulder, giving it a squeeze.

"Right then. One more, mate, just you and me. Then I'd better get a taxi out of here. Harold mate, one more thing? Just... be careful with this psychology bird, yeah?"

Harry sighed.

"Yeah. I will."

Chapter 15

Harry's stomach growled in anticipation of his morning cinnamon swirl as he approached the office, the practice all but ritualistic by now. Definitely needed to call that gym.

"Morning, Harry!" Olivia beamed, jumping up to greet him.

"Good morning! This is the part where you tell me I have no whiskey barrels today, and we've just been given a winning lottery ticket by a passing raven?"

Olivia giggled, covering her mouth.

"That's unusually creative, Harry! You must be in a good mood. I'll keep that up by telling you that no, you don't have a single whiskey barrel to deal with today!"

Olivia started dancing on the spot. Harry, moved by her display, joined her—for just a brief moment, or two.

The roof firmly raised, he strolled past into his office, utterly devastated.

"No... No swirls today?"

Olivia followed him in, frowning, patting his gut.

"You've had a few too many of those lately, Harry. But there are chopped vegetables instead, and cucumber sandwiches."

Harry sighed, then nodded his head slightly. It was sweet of her to care, though he felt like a baby robbed of his candy.

"You're probably right. This is a psychologist's office, not a bakery. And I have gained a little... pudge, lately."

Harry grabbed at his soft, flabby belly, making Olivia giggle.

"Well, just makes you more cuddly, Harry. OK, let's get to work! Oh, and Harry? I'm really looking forward to tonight."

Oh no. He hadn't agreed to anything at all, had he?

Oh... she was referring to sword practice, which would be great fun. Great, ethical fun.

"Should be ethical. Um, fun, I mean. Swords are cathartic! Great fun being clad in armour."

Olivia giggled. "Now there's an idea for a casual Friday. I'll send your first client in when they get here."

Olivia carefully closed the door behind her with a gentle click.

Harry checked his phone to find a text from Jester.

"Harry my guy, you're taking Tim down tonight. I can feel it. There's an electricity in the air, man. Tonight's the night. Peace."

Harry smiled, gently flipping the phone with his fingers. Jester had his moments, but he still brought Harry warmth.

Lunchtime rolled around again quickly enough, clients served, more emails drafted, work done for the day. Thursdays were always slow and steady, but they helped offset the pace of frantic Fridays and manic Mondays.

Olivia gently pushed open the door, Tupperware in hand.

"Check it out, Harry! Chicken salad for you."

Harry shook his head. "I was thinking more Chinese, to be honest, Olivia. I haven't had a spring roll in ages."

Olivia glared a little, narrowing her gaze.

"Come on, Harry. I made this special for you. Besides, that's a lot of calories."

Harry sighed, slumping in his chair, stomach gurgling. "I am hungry, and you're probably right. Need to fit in my armour, don't I. Thanks, Olivia."

She beamed a smile, handing Harry the fork and salad, followed by her happy little claps.

Certainly not as fun as a sugary swirl, but probably healthier. Still tasted like ash.

"I've been working on my digital design skills, Harry! I drew you a little penguin. Animated him, too. Remember that AI gadget I showed you for transcription? I found others, too. One that can animate my drawings. Isn't that great?"

Harry spun his phone in his hand, eyes fixed firmly on Olivia, but ears elsewhere.

"Oh that's lovely, Olivia. I haven't been to see that penguin exhibit at the sea life centre yet. I should do that. Say, are you ready for swords tonight?"

Olivia folded her arms across her chest, looking at her feet. "Yeah, I think so. Bit nervous, Harry. Will you take care of me? You can be my knight in shining armour."

Harry chuckled, sitting upright in his chair, adjusting his tie. "Yes, of course we'll all be there to support you, Olivia. Do you have a lift?"

"Jester said your brother will collect me on the way! He's called Tim, right? Is he a looker like you, Harry?"

Harry gripped at his tie.

"Oh dear. He certainly likes to think so. I'm sure his wife does, too. Well, lunchtime's over. Back to it."

Well, swords tonight wouldn't be a bore, Harry was sure of that.

Chapter 16

Harry groaned, hauling his kit bag into the boot of his car before climbing inside. Phone buzzed.

"Do enjoy your little sword play tonight, darling. Don't do anything I wouldn't do. Harriet x"

Harry sighed, staring through the phone.

If she were trying to scam him, she was lousy at it. No demands, no *"oh no, something bad happened and I need money"*, just conversation. Mostly academic, but hinting at something hidden beneath.

Phone back in his pocket, the hum of the tyres pleasing to his ear. Soon, the boys would be together again, steel on steel, in their biblical arena.

Oh, right. The boys and Olivia. Bugger.

Harry sighed, gripping the wheel a little tighter.

Moments later, he pulled up at the church, the others... already inside?

Harry froze, hurriedly fumbling in his pockets for the church key. He felt the foreboding, cold ancient iron of the key in his hand, clearly still there.

Someone else must have one now, then.

Harry clambered out of his car, hauling the kit bag onto his shoulder with a groan. He slammed the boot shut and meandered over to the others.

"Yo! Harry! My guy!" Jester yelled out at Harry, spotting him enter. The echoes of steel ringing out in the hallowed halls ceased on his approach.

Harry dropped his kit bag onto the front pew with a wooden thud from beneath. Olivia was sitting nearby, wearing a tight white dress, impractical for wielding a blade.

Wore plenty of makeup for a night of sword-filled mayhem.

Simon folded his arms, nodding to Harry, Tim clambering over for a hug, panting.

"Harry mate! Olly here got a key from the vicar. Anyway, how are you?"

Harry hugged his brother back tight.

"Good to see you all. It's been a good day, I—"

"Certainly has, Harry! We had fun at work, didn't we?" Olivia interjected.

He nodded, carefully removing the cold, heavy metal garb from his bag.

"Harry, can you give me a hand, please?"

Olivia gestured towards her kit bag, unzipped, armour inside.

"None of you offered to help the poor girl?" Harry said, eyes accusing the room.

Simon simply shrugged.

"Well, she ain't letting me anywhere near her, Harry, but I think we creep each other out a bit, don't we love?" Jester said, earning himself a scowl from Olivia.

"Gotta be you, mate, Olly said so herself. She trusts you, Harry," Tim added.

Harry shrugged, carefully removing armour pieces from Olivia's kit bag, the majority of his own worn first. Her armour was ornate and beautiful, including a full set of greaves and breastplate to match.

The glint of the dim church lights and the full moon beaming through the stained glass window reflected off the ornate patterns on her armour. Harry carefully helped Olivia into each and every piece, fastening the leather straps in place with care.

Harry wiped a bead of sweat from his brow, gazing at Olivia, proudly standing wearing her ornate armour. Stunning.

The silence was deafening. Harry quickly scanned the room, heart pounding, noticing all eyes were on him.

"Bloody hell, Harry. Should I book you two a room?" Jester mocked, finally breaking the silence.

Simon chuckled a little, arms still folded, smile curling up in his weathered cheeks.

"Right, well, if you're quite ready, Harry mate, it's time we suit you and I boot you. You won't be beating me tonight, no matter what this joker says," Tim declared, pointing a gauntlet towards Jester.

"Harry, how do I look?" Olivia asked, beaming a hopeful smile.

"Your armour is radiant—absolutely beautiful, even. Wherever did you find it?"

"Oh... Well, a medieval market, actually. Takes a while to get there, especially on buses, but it was lovely. We should go some time, Harry!"

Olivia clapped her metal gauntlets together a little, fumbling in her new armour.

"Oh, um. I also have something for you. A present!"

Olivia reached into her kit bag, pulling out a sword. She held it by the scabbard with both hands, offering the hilt to Harry.

Harry's eyes widened, shaking in his armour.

"Uh... What's this?"

Once more, Harry felt the familiar gaze of all eyes on him—or at least, the blade.

"Medieval English-style longsword, more fitting for a man of your height than a Viking broadsword. I made sure it suited your height perfectly. Draw it, Harry. It's yours."

Harry's heart beat fast, chest tightening, stares and silence overbearing. They needed to stop. They had to stop. He had to draw the sword.

He shook as he touched the blade, pulling it from the scabbard with both hands. It was stunning, a finely crafted piece of forged metal, shining in the light of the moon. He gripped it with both hands, held it high. The weight of it pulled against his wrist a little, but it was magnificent.

This felt like more than just a sword.

Harry quickly slid the blade back into the scabbard. "Olivia, this can't have been cheap. You were so kind, but I'm not sure I can accept this. Besides—where is your blade?"

Olivia started giggling, metal from her armour rattling a little. "Knew you'd say that. So I propose a deal, dear Harry. With the fancy new longsword, you can trade me for your old Viking broadsword, then we both have a fitting weapon."

Harry shook his head. "Ah, no. Tim bought me that. I can't."

Tim interjected, finally. "Mate, you bloody stupid? Look at that thing. Come on, make the trade already, and let's fight. You're going down, new sword, old sword— any sword."

Almost felt like giving away Mr Snuffles, handing his broadswords to Olivia with a frown.

Harry closed his eyes and took a deep breath, Tim carefully securing his helmet to his head.

Harry pulled the longsword from the scabbard, the satisfying sound of metal scraping against the worn leather inside, tossing the scabbard onto the pew. It was heavy, pulling against his wrist, so he gripped it tightly with both hands, knuckles whitening.

Simon smirked, quite possibly imagining Harry and his new longsword taking on his zweihander.

Harry placed the sword down onto the pew, securing his helmet on his head, breathing quickening inside. The weight of the helmet ached against his neck, as the others stepped aside, watching intently.

Longsword back in hand, Harry and Tim took the field. The hallowed halls felt different somehow, smaller, closing in on Harry. He sighed, ready to duel his brother once more.

"All right, boys. Tonight's the night. Harry's finally gonna beat Tim, I can feel it. You feel it, boys?"

Jester was practically bouncing on the spot, ready to marshal.

"I bloody don't. You're going down, Harry, same as usual, mate. Let's do this."

"Lay on arms! Fight!" Jester yelled, swords raised.

Harry swung his longsword in a wide arc, the weight of it gnawing at his wrists. Tim effortlessly intercepted the blow, the sound of steel on steel ringing out in the biblical battlefield.

Tim came at Harry from above, but he nimbly stepped back, armoured feet clunking on the wood beneath.

"Use your reach, Harry!" Jester called out, smacked in the arm by Simon. Olivia's metallic little claps screamed inside Harry's ears, reverberating through the helmet.

Harry gripped the hilt of his blade tightly, swinging high, Tim barely evading the head blow.

The echoes of steel on steel rang out to the heavens in the hallowed halls for quite some time, the boys panting. Harry intercepted a head blow from Tim, steel scraping against steel, countering with a sweep for Tim's arm, blade meeting pauldron.

"Fight!" Jester yelled. "Hell yes, Harry! My guy!" Everyone gathered round the boys, the fight having concluded in Harry's favour. Olivia crashed against him, metal on metal, hugging him tightly.

She pulled away, her hand lingering on his pauldron a beat. Her eyes bright, intense beneath the joy. Giggled and bounced away as his chest heaved.

His helmet felt hot, heavy, breathing laboured inside. He discarded his sword, quickly pulled off the helm and placed it on the pew with a thunk on the wood below. Harry flopped next to it, Tim joining him, arm round his brother's pauldrons.

They both panted heavily, drawing short, sharp breaths.

Simon and Jester wasted no time, helmets affixed, preparing for their own biblical battle.

"Harold mate. Well done, well done mate, you earned that win."

Tim paused, panting a little more, before continuing.

"Bloody hell, gonna have to adjust my tactics now you've got a new blade."

Tim patted him on the back, sprang to his feet and prepared to marshal. Simon was practically rabid, gripping his zweihander so tightly the hilt almost screamed under the pressure.

Olivia replaced Tim on the pew, patting Harry on the leg with her gauntleted hand.

"You did so well, Harry! Will you teach me now?"

Harry shook his head. "Sorry, these two are about to duel. Can't miss that."

Olivia slumped on the pew a little, folding her arms across her ornate breastplate.

"Lay on arms!" Tim called out, Simon wasting no time at all, bringing his massive sword down on Jester's head with a roar. The steel cried out, echoing and singing through the halls as Jester deftly blocked it with both blades in a cross.

Harry watched intently, steel clashing and scraping against steel, music to his ears, his soul.

"Can't we just practise over there on the other side, Harry?" Olivia asked, shattering the spell.

"Not missing this bout. Watch them, they're magnificent!"

Olivia rolled her eyes, walking off to the other side of the church, broadsword in sheath by her side.

"Fight over!" Tim called, Jester raising his swords up high, a sly smack on the greaves stealing him victory.

Simon growled through heavy breaths, discarding his sword, thudding against the carpet.

"Simon, bruv, you snooze, you lose!" Jester taunted.

They both chuckled and hugged through laboured breaths, Olivia off to the side, broadsword drawn.

"Come on then, Olly, I'll show you how it's done, mate," Tim said as he drew his broadsword once more, beckoning her over with a gauntlet.

"Can't Harry do it? I trust him."

Tim shrugged, handing his broadsword to Harry, church walls edging closer as he took the hilt.

Helm affixed, Harry rose to his feet, ready to teach Olivia the basics of blocks and strikes.

He approached Olivia, heat inside his helm rising to a furnace. The broadsword felt like an extension of his arm, almost a perfect facsimile of his—now Olivia's—broadsword. Bugger.

"Feet shoulder-width apart, stand firm. Like this," Harry commanded, Olivia eagerly following suit.

"Think of the blade as an extension of your arm, your will, not a foreign object. The weight will feel heavy, pulling against your wrist at first. But over time, it'll feel natural, feel right."

She copied Harry, almost perfectly, mimicking his instructions.

"Keep your elbow up, Olly!" Tim called out from the pew where the others were watching.

Olivia looked to Harry for approval. He mimicked the suggested movement and she copied along.

"We'll practise blocking now. I'm starting to tire though, maybe Tim can tag in?"

Olivia shook her head. "You're my teacher, Harry!"

"We're a brotherhood, Olivia. We all teach and inspire one another. Brothers in steel!"

"Brothers in steel!" the other men parroted back, echoing through the halls of the church.

Olivia shrugged, rolling her eyes. "I just feel like I learn better from you, that's all. OK, you rest on the bench. Can you help me, Tim?"

Tim groaned, rising to his feet. "Sure thing, Olly. Right then, blocking."

Olivia copied Tim as best she could, offering fleeting glances towards Harry as time allowed.

"Yo, Harry, Simon and I came up with an idea for the castle. You gonna love this, trust. So Simon here, takes on both you boys at once, two blades versus his zweihander. He's ready. You are, too."

Harry gazed over at his former broadsword, frowning a little. "I'll need to borrow a smaller blade back, but it sounds like fun."

Steel clashed against steel, echoing out into the night. It soon came time to pack up and go home.

"Can I have a lift please, Harry?" Olivia suggested meekly.

"Didn't Tim bring you?" he retorted, turning to his brother.

"Sorry, mate, gotta collect Yvette, the boys and her mum. You sort it, I'll text ya. Right, later, boys." Tim headed off, Simon and Jester quickly following suit, leaving Harry and Olivia alone in the church.

"That was lovely, Harry. Thank you," Olivia said, beaming a smile.

Harry hauled the kit bags carefully into the boot, leaving Olivia to lock the ancient oak doors.

The drive to Olivia's home was accompanied by comfortable silence, mixed with the scent of strawberries and armour polish. Street lights flickered across her face as they pulled up to the run-down block of flats, the roof tile still hanging on for dear life.

Harry hauled her heavy kit bag from the boot to her ground-floor flat, carefully dropping it onto the sofa inside. The colours quickly overwhelmed his tiring senses, as he gazed forlornly at the kit bag with his former broadsword inside.

Olivia kissed Harry on the cheek, her lips warm against his face. "Thank you for a lovely evening, Harry. Would you like to stay for a coffee?"

Not bloody likely.

"Far too knackered. Night Olivia."

Olivia smiled, waving furiously at him as he left, wiping his cheek with his hand as the door closed.

Lines felt a little blurrier tonight. On the drive home, Harry tapped the wheel ceaselessly.

Chapter 17

"Morning, Harry!" Olivia beamed from her desk as he stepped into the lobby, straightening his tie.

"Good morning. Hope you had a good time last night. What's on the agenda for today, then?"

Olivia frowned, brushing her shoulder. "Whiskey barrel scams. Lots, and lots of them."

Harry's heart sank, shoulders slumping. He loosened his tie once more.

"Kidding! You have a cryptocurrency scam this morning."

Harry narrowed his gaze. "Right, well, send them in when ready. Thanks, Olivia."

As he creaked open his office door, his nose was once again treated to the smell of sugary sweet cinnamon, along with chopped carrot.

He leaned his head back out of the door. "The swirls are back?"

Olivia scowled. "One, Harry! The rest are for your clients."

Harry frowned and shuffled over to his desk, gently running a finger along the soft, flaky pastry of his cinnamon swirl. There were a dozen of them, all calling out to him, begging to be consumed, but his tongue would have to settle with just the one dancing away on his taste buds.

Harry shook his head and turned his attention to his text messages.

"Morning, darling. I hope you had a lovely time at sword practice last night. I do love to imagine the imagery of you in a suit of armour, even if it's not my thing. Have a grand day. Call this week?
Harriet x"

Harry popped the phone back into his pocket and gazed over at the bookshelf, drumming his fingers on the mahogany desk. A thought occurred to him—he could acquire a book she'd written, and have a discussion about it on their first call.

The intercom buzzed, jolting him upright.

"Sending in Barry Temple now, Harry."

Tale of woe about cryptocurrency investment, which was pretty common. Absolute breeding ground for scammers, and rarely reimbursed.

Olivia popped into the office, lunchtime.

"Well, I'm definitely ready for lunch, that's for sure. Why don't we order that Chinese?"

Olivia folded her arms and shook her head, before producing a Tupperware container of chicken salad from the fridge.

Harry sighed, beginning to wonder who was actually in charge here. Still, she was kind enough to make it for him, and it was lunch, though wouldn't taste like it. Might actually get more joy from eating bark.

"So, swords last night was great fun, wasn't it, Harry! Did you like your new blade?"

Harry sighed, loosening his tie.

"It certainly helped me beat my brother. It was very kind, Olivia, but are you sure it was appropriate? It can't have been cheap."

Olivia's smile faltered.

"You don't like it, Harry?"

Harry shook his head. "I just mean, it's quite the gesture, that's all—I have to admit, it did feel a little awkward accepting it. I need to be honest about that."

Olivia smiled.

"Well, get used to it. You deserve the best, Harry. Now you've beaten your brother, maybe you can beat the ogre and the buffoon, too! Harry, champion knight of the realm!"

Harry chuckled nervously. Those names seemed a little unkind. Still, all in good fun.

"So Harry, how goes your dating app then? Any lovely ladies on there?"

The question pressed at him, Harry feeling his tie choke him a little. He pulled the damned thing off, loosening his top button, carelessly dropping it on the desk.

"Not so much. I've taken a bit of a break from it, I suppose. A doctor of psychology, but I feel more like she's studying me than anything—and we haven't even had a video call or a date in person at all. For all I know, could be a particularly inept scammer. Maybe I should try harder, meet someone else."

Olivia grinned, grabbing a cinnamon swirl. "She sounds lovely, Harry. Well, lunch is over. Bye, Harry!"

Olivia grabbed her empty Tupperware, salad reluctantly crunched by Harry. Genuinely might have to try that bark to compare the taste.

She closed the door gently behind her.

He glared at the closed door, the echo of lunch lingering. Something about the exchange tied a knot in his stomach, left him feeling hollow.

His phone buzzed, a text from Harriet.

"Why don't we have a call after work, darling? Say eight? Harriet x"

For the first time in a while, he found himself looking forward to something that had nothing to do with swords, scams, or strawberry-scented secretaries. Hopefully, no trunks necessary.

Chapter 18

A nervous energy crackled through the air that night. Even Mr Snuffles seemed anxious.

Harry ran his fingers through his hair, freshly washed, still not feeling clean. He'd worked up a sweat as he tidied frantically, hoovered up, straightened the pictures—effort Harriet wouldn't see.

Why was his pulse racing? Just a phone call, that's all. Did hundreds of these during those dreaded days in the trenches of customer service.

He fired up his laptop, searching online for articles and books by Dr Harriet Baker. Her latest article appeared to be titled '*Psychological manipulation in digital spaces*', which he brought up and began to scan. Her writing was brilliant, insightful, showing a depth of understanding about human vulnerability that matched—or likely exceeded—his own.

Harry connected his Bluetooth headset to his phone and lay next to Mr Snuffles on his warm, comfy bed.

Five past eight. He was even being stood up on a phone call now. That settled it, time to wash the swimming trunks.

Moments later, his phone suddenly buzzed, startling him so badly he almost fell off the bed. The screen showed a number with no caller ID.

"Hello?" His voice came out higher than intended. He cleared his throat, grabbing a nearby glass of water.

"Harry, darling? It's Harriet."

Her voice was warm, slightly husky, with that unavoidable Norfolk twang.

"Ha! I was beginning to think you'd stood me up on a phone call." He winced, gripping his glass of water hard.

She laughed, the sound resonating through his chest. "So sorry, you know how it is. Always something needing your attention."

"Too true," he said, settling onto the side of the bed. "It's lovely to finally hear your voice. Personally, I mean—I've seen some of your lectures online."

"Likewise, darling. I've been looking forward to this all day. I'm glad you can hear me appropriately."

The conversation flowed with surprising ease. They discussed her paper first—Harry had highlighted several passages that particularly resonated with his own work, and she seemed genuinely impressed by his insights.

"In my research, under the right circumstances, victims of financial fraud are given a freeing choice. They have nothing left to lose, and can rebuild themselves completely, from the ground up. Fascinating, isn't it?"

Harry smiled at the ceiling a moment before responding.

"I can't discuss specific clients, I'm sure you'll understand, but I've seen similar patterns in my work. Some of my clients have transformed after their ordeals—some notably more successful than before! It just goes to show, humanity endures."

"There's an elegance to it, isn't there? Morally reprehensible, of course, but psychologically fascinating."

Harry nodded before remembering she couldn't see him. "Absolutely. I'm constantly amazed by how well scammers understand human psychology without any formal training—they're natural behaviourists. Did you read my article comparing the psychology of sales to scams? It's essentially the same skill set."

"Shifting the subject slightly, darling," Harriet said, her voice settling to a softer tone, "you mentioned your childhood in our texts. You said you lived with your aunt after your parents died?"

Harry hesitated. He looked to his bunny, almost seeking approval. "Yes. Plane crash when I was a teen. Tim was eight."

"I'm so sorry, darling. What a terrible thing for a child to experience."

"It was... difficult. I don't talk about it much."

"And your aunt raised you both?"

"No, actually. We were separated. I went to live with her in Hunstanton, Tim with our uncle in Norwich. Different lives, but we saw each other at weekends from time to time."

"That separation must have been traumatic in its own way," Harriet said softly. "Losing your parents and then being separated from your brother."

Harry sighed, reaching to straighten his tie and finding only the fabric of his T-shirt. "I suppose it was. I've never really thought about it much. I have my family now, and they're everything to me."

"Children are remarkably resilient, but those early experiences shape us in profound ways."

Harry felt himself unravelling a tad.

"I was always the responsible one, even before they died. Mum used to call me her 'darling boy.' With my aunt I felt I had to be perfect—never cause problems, never be a burden. Times I felt like a guest."

"And guests have to earn their keep, don't they? Found yourself being useful before you were asked. Made yourself easy to be around. That hypervigilance becomes exhausting, always monitoring your value."

Bugger. Nail right on the head.

"And you endured all this, whilst your brother got to remain a child?" Harriet concluded.

Harry tapped his fingers against the water glass.

"Yes. Exactly that."

The conversation flowed from there into deeper waters. Harry found himself telling her about the sleepless nights after his parents died, about Mr Snuffles being his only confidant, about the academic achievements that never quite filled the void, that his parents never got to see.

"I'm sorry," he said finally, realising he'd been talking about himself for nearly ten whole minutes. "This wasn't exactly what I had in mind for our first call."

"Don't apologise," Harriet said warmly. "I find you fascinating, Harry. Your resilience, your compassion for scam victims—it all makes perfect sense now. Look how you rebuilt yourself after all you went through—a survivor, through and through."

"Should we use video?" Harry ventured.

"Ah," she sighed. "My internet connection is awful tonight. I'm actually calling from my mobile because my Wi-Fi keeps dropping. Rural Norfolk isn't known for its technological infrastructure, is it?"

"Perhaps we should discuss more of our psychological work over coffee sometime?"

"I'd love that," she said. "Though I'm buried in research at the moment. End of term is approaching, and the department expects a new paper by the end of the month."

"I understand."

Harry smiled, closing his eyes. He'd verified her credentials, her academics, her works. Still, was she avoiding something, or genuinely just busy? University professor likely had an incredibly busy schedule.

"Hmm. So you mentioned a secretary, an Olivia. What's she like?"

Harry paused a moment. "Young. Eager. Very capable at work. Perhaps a bit too intense, sometimes."

"Intense how?"

"She goes the extra mile, she really does. Not sometimes, but all the time. She brings me lunch daily, knows my schedule far better than I do, seems to anticipate everything I need. Honestly, I've truly come to depend on her—perhaps, even, to a fault."

"She certainly sounds devoted, darling. Have you considered she may see you as more than a boss?" Harriet observed.

"It isn't like that. She's young, smart, charming and honestly, if I were ten years younger and not her boss, sure. But that isn't the reality, and I've accepted that—as has she."

There was a long pause before Harriet responded.

"If you say so, darling."

The conversation moved on to other topics. Harry found himself laughing more than he had in months, delighting in her sharp wit and thoughtful insights.

"Oh wow," Harriet said suddenly. "Is that the time? We've been chatting for nearly two hours!"

"I had no idea," he responded.

"Time flies when you're having fun," she said, her voice warm. "I haven't enjoyed a conversation this much in ages, Harry. Same time next week? And perhaps I can get my camera working by then."

"Perfect."

"Goodnight then, darling. Sweet dreams."

"Sweet dreams, Harriet."

Chapter 19

Saturday rolled around, and it was typically a break from the wailing screeches of Barbie Girl.

Not today, however—there was a long road ahead to the forge experience day in Lincolnshire.

The flyer had sat pinned to Harry's noticeboard for quite literally years, taken from his first medieval event. About bloody time.

Showering seemed almost pointless with the sweaty, molten heat they were about to endure and enjoy in equal measure.

Harry's phone buzzed with a message in the group chat.

> *"Brothers in steel! Are we ready to smack an anvil like proper blacksmiths of old?"*

> *"Coffee."*

> *"Settle down, mates. Now leaving Norwich.*
> *Harold, you better be ready!"*

Harry rushed to get ready, grabbing a cinnamon swirl from the fridge that he'd nabbed from work the day before. He took his time, savouring the sugary sweet cinnamon sensation—so different from the hurried, guilty crunch at his desk yesterday.

The scent of strawberry lingered in his mind for just a moment once more, as he finished the flaky pastry.

Harry stepped outside adorned in a loose vest and shorts. A brisk, cool stroll along the promenade filled his lungs with fresh salty sea air once more.

Harry checked his phone to find a text from Harriet.

"Do enjoy your weekend, Harry. Looking forward to our video call next week, darling. Harriet x"

He pocketed the phone, deciding to reply later. He was practically buzzing with energy, despite the poor sleep, feeling the heat from the forge in his mind's eye.

Harry made his way back home, Tim and the others waiting in the car out front.

"Bloody hell, Harold, we've been here a good ten minutes. Where were you?"

Harry hopped in the front passenger seat and belted up. "Sorry all, got some fresh air. Brisk walk to wake me up."

"Harry, bruv, I'm liking the look— but ain't you cold in that vest?"

Harry smirked. "Ask me again when we're at the forge."

Jester's grin sank as he looked down at his black sweatshirt.

Harry pulled out his phone, tapping a reply to Harriet.

"Thank you! Off to Spalding with the boys today. Forging some steel. Enjoy your weekend, Harry."

He slipped his phone back in his pocket, but Tim couldn't help but notice, his gaze faltering from the road.

"Harry mate, finally got a bird on the go?" he stated bluntly.

"No, not really. Just a psychology doctor I'm talking to, from the University of East Anglia. It's interesting, but I'm not sure about it."

Tim bashed the middle of the steering wheel, honking at a particularly slow tractor almost in the middle of the road.

"Just you be careful, mate, lot of them scammers about."

The brothers shared a small chuckle as a thread of doubt dared to unravel in Harry's mind.

"Yeah, I know. Thanks, Tim. I'm being careful—we're having a video call next week, and there's talk of a coffee date."

Tim grinned, gripping the wheel a little looser. "Good, mate. Little hard for her to scam you in person, isn't it?"

"Oh I dunno, bruv, she could be one of them chicks with dicks, innit!" Jester jibed from the back, quickly regretting it as Simon smacked him in the arm.

"Compassion," he declared, like a decree, Jester rolling his eyes.

"Right, mates, I'm pulling over for coffees. Harry's buying."

Harry raised an eyebrow, beginning to wonder when this group had acquired such agency over his wallet as they pulled into the service station.

"Well... Guess you're paying for the petrol, aren't you, Timothy? Of course, happy to. Crisps or anything, gents?"

"Quavers!" Simon boomed from the back, Jester holding up two fingers and grinning.

"Right, two packets of crisps for you two, and some chocolate for Tim. That right?"

Tim grinned widely. "Harold, you know me so well. Chop chop, mate. I'm fuelling up, so you can buy that too."

Harry sighed, glaring a little at Tim, soon disarmed by the hearty chuckles of all three brothers.

Harry pushed against the cold glass door of the service station, greeted by the shelves stacked with junk food and assorted appliances. Up at the counter, he noticed someone familiar.

"Mr Harry!" Sareth beamed from behind the counter, attending the till.

Harry's joy was hard to contain. It was incredibly rare to see a client out in the real world, much less one who used to be a Cambodian indentured compound scammer.

"Sareth, so delightful to see you. So you're working now? How's that going?"

"Oh Mr Harry, I'm doing good. Very good, yes. I work here part-time, and I take the course for computers! I see your secretary too, when we meet Sunday for the course. I'm learning so much information technology. You helped me so much. Thank you, thank you thank you! I write the book too—as we discuss."

"Oh, that's wonderful. Olivia loves to study, I'm almost not surprised to hear she's taking the course too. It was good to see you, Sareth, truly. See you soon."

"Yes, very helpful, Mr Harry. Smart girl. Well, you safe journey now, yes? Bye bye! Oh after pay, of course!"

Harry and Sareth both chuckled, Harry tapping the plastic and back to the car.

"Harry, bruv, that your best mate in there or what? We been waiting ages here!" Jester jabbed from the back.

"Client of mine, lovely guy. He's writing a book actually, about his time in a scamming compound in Cambodia. I wouldn't usually share such information, but he's allowed me to, since he's writing about it."

Jester mimicked a yawn. "That was a bloody book, Harry. Scammer you say? Do I need to check my pockets?"

Simon smacked Jester in the arm once more. "Compassion," he echoed firmly.

"He was trafficked, actually. Fascinating as it is heartbreaking. Cambodian scammer compounds—they lure in victims, force them to scam. If they don't meet targets, the lash of the whip is their reward."

The mood in the car shifted, the energy in the air still.

"Jesus, mate," Tim muttered. "I thought car sales was rough. Still, I'd make a lot more sales with a whip at me back."

Jester cracked up in the back, laughing like a hyena, quickly silenced by a third smack from Simon.

"Simon, bruv, chill! That's my forging arm!" Jester snapped, still grinning.

"Not long now, boys. You all excited?"

"Claymore!" Simon roared from the back.

Harry took that as a yes.

They pulled up in front of an old, weathered building on the outskirts of Spalding, bricks decaying and worn, cracks in the foundation.

The black wooden doors swung open to reveal a brute of a man, grey beard that would give Gandalf himself envy.

His muscles glistened with sweat, huge and swollen—even Simon was in awe.

"Welcome! Welcome, boys. Max, the forgemaster."

He pointed at Harry.

"Smart one, here. You'll soon warm up in there, son, don't you worry about that."

He turned his gaze to Simon.

"Bloody hell, big man. You sure you haven't worked a forge before? Look at the size of you!"

"Lorry mechanic," Simon simply stated.

"Love me a man who knows the value of hard work. Right then, boys, follow me—we've a hard day's graft ahead of us."

The boys followed him inside, heat from the forge hitting them like a wave even against the bigger chill of the autumn air outside.

Tools of various shapes and sizes hung on the walls, anvils stationed at four workbenches around the furnace, pumping heat in waves from the middle of the room.

"Right, boys," Max announced, voice booming over the roaring flames. "Fun we shall have, but safe fun it shall be. Anyone worked the forge before?"

The boys looked at one another, all shaking their heads.

"Listen well. Respect the forge and the flame. This is no game. Mistakes cost you in here. This wicked scar on my side here? It's no tattoo."

All four of their gazes met his finger, showing an incredible burn scar on his abdomen.

"Watch, and learn." Max grabbed a series of tools, demonstrating the basics—heating the metal until it glowed, how to strike it properly with the blacksmith hammer, how to quench it in the water bucket with a satisfying hiss.

"Now, what are we making today, lads?" Max asked, clapping his massive hands together.

"Claymore!" Simon bellowed immediately, above the roaring flame.

Max chuckled. "Ambitious! Let's do it! The rest of you?"

"Short sword," Tim decided, glancing at Harry.

"Same here," Harry agreed.

"Can I do two daggers?" Jester asked. "One for each hand, like my fighting style."

"Well, you may try," Max said sceptically. "Could be biting off more than you can chew, son, but I admire the spirit."

He assigned them each to a station, Simon taking the largest anvil without question. He worked effortlessly, as if born of the forge, a mountain of a man born out of time.

"One day isn't enough to fully complete your weapons," Max explained, selecting metal blanks from a shelf. "Forging and shaping our blades is the goal today, and I'll finish the tempering and handle-fitting during the week. Steel ready for collection next Friday."

Something primal stirred in Harry, the pulsing, beating, rhythmic clanging of hammers against anvils. He found himself lost in the process, almost meditating, the focused, laborious nature of it clearing his mind, freeing him of thought. There was something honest about it— the metal responded exactly as it should to his efforts, not a scam in sight. Needed to feel something real.

Max moved between them, offering guidance and corrections, as the boys worked hard.

During a break to let their arms recover and the metal cool, they gathered around a bench where Max had laid out water bottles.

"Harry mate," Tim began, wiping sweat from his brow, "swords felt a bit weird on Thursday, didn't it? The usual energy just felt a bit different, bit intense maybe."

"You're starting to sound like Jester, Timothy. Speak plainly."

A little plain-spoken for Harry himself, but the dull ache of his muscles from the hammering had dulled his usual careful demeanour.

"Olly seems a bit intense is all. Think she's got a hard on for you mate."

Simon laughed hard, before draining the rest of his water bottle, crushing it in his massive paw.

"Harry, bruv, she's proper into you. Just watch yourself. I don't dig her energy, you feel me?" Jester added.

Harry smirked. "You're just salty because she rejected you, Jester. Don't give me that. Besides, it isn't like that—we're colleagues and professionals."

"All right, yeah I'm salty, but still, just watch yourself. I don't want things getting weird with the brothers in steel! Maybe we need a no chicks policy?"

Simon smacked Jester in the arm again. "Show compassion!"

"Christ, Simon, that's two words. You better calm yourself down Jester," Tim warned.

Break was over, the fiery flame of the forge roaring beside them all once more, as they once again took hammer to molten steel. The rest of the day passed in a volcanic blur of radiating heat and flame.

Salty sweat drenching their clothes and thoroughly exhausted, the boys were aching in muscles they didn't know they had.

The five blades in their rudimentary form were finally ready, surrendered into the care of the forgemaster.

"You boys have done yourselves proud. Especially you, young man, your daggers are fine indeed. Well, it's been a pleasure having you all. Come collect your steel next Friday. God bless."

Max waved them off, as they set off once more for the charming seaside town of Hunstanton. Harry tried his best to focus on the road, but found himself pondering a certain secretary instead.

Chapter 20

"Harry mate, cheers for letting us borrow your shower," Tim said as he plonked the tray of beers down on the table in the corner of the beer garden.

"Of course, saved you a trip back to Norwich, and let you get a beer. Just the one, Timothy, since you're driving."

"Yes, Dad," Tim retorted, smirking.

"I gotta say though, boys," Jester began, gesturing to Simon, "bit weird seeing the big man here without overalls on. Jesus, bruv, look at them arms!"

Jester gave Simon's arm a squeeze, as he carelessly drained his pint as if Jester wasn't there.

"Christ, Jester, buy the man dinner first. Anyway, mates, that was bloody unforgettable. I'm shattered—not even the wife can wear me out like that!"

Simon heaved his heavy chest, grumbling with laughter, Jester offering Tim a high five.

Harry grabbed his phone, checking his notifications.

"Harry, your subscription has expired."

He stared off at the lamp on the rear of the pub, flipping his phone in his hand. He sighed, tapping into it, opting for another month of romantic misery.

He quickly stuffed the phone back into his pocket, as he noticed a familiar face enter the beer garden.

"Hi Harry!" Olivia waved, skipping quickly over and pulling up a chair next to him.

"Good to see you, Olivia. More cover shifts?" Harry asked.

"Yep! Two hours, but you know me, Harry, always early."

Harry gazed off at the lampshade once more.

"I can't bloody wait for next Friday, boys. I can already feel those daggers in my hands, running rings round Si. You're going down, bruv!" Jester mocked.

"Oh that's right! You went to the forge! So how was that, then, Harry?" Olivia asked.

"I don't recall mentioning it. I may well have let it slip at lunchtime, I've been bubbling with anticipation over it. It was hard work, but so very much worth it. Our forgemaster, Max, was impeccable."

Simon raised his second pint to that, draining half.

"Oh! That reminds me. There's a medieval market event happening tomorrow, up in Coventry. Quite a distance, I know, but you drive, Harry, and it would be so much fun. The forgemaster there, Master Preston, will put your Max to shame."

Simon grunted. "Impossible," draining the rest of his pint.

"I think I should know, thank you. He made Harry's longsword, perfectly specified to his needs. And why don't you talk much, anyway? It's creepy!"

Tim and Jester glared at Olivia, but Simon simply shrugged and chuckled to himself.

"Why waste words?" he decreed.

Man would make a fine poet.

"Sorry, Simon, I didn't mean to snap like that. Just a lot on my mind. The medieval market tomorrow will have all sorts of fun! There's armour, weapons, crafts and jewellery—oh and period food, too!"

Jester's frown turned upside down. "Ohhh, now you've got my attention, missy. Food ya say? C'mon, boys, let's hit it. What time, Olly?"

"Starts at ten, so we'll need to leave by about seven."

Bugger. Another weekend dose of Barbie Girl.

"Overtime," Simon barked, folding his arms across his chest.

"I'm in, Harold. I'll drive to you, picking Olly up, and the four of us will go. Sound good, mate?"

"Can't Harry pick me up too? I want to make sure my outfit is period-appropriate before I leave my flat," Olivia interjected.

"Don't worry, Olivia, Tim can answer that too. Right then, it's settled. Off to the medieval market tomorrow. It won't be the same without you though, Simon," Harry said as he patted Simon on the shoulder, met by his giant paw.

Olivia clapped, standing to leave. "Lovely. OK, I'll go inside. Bye, Harry!"

She skipped off towards the door, leaving the group in awkward silence for a moment in her absence.

Jester was the first to stick a dagger in the tension. "Well that was bloody rude, innit? Simon minding his own business, she tears him a new one. She on shark week or something?"

Simon smacked Jester in the arm.

"She did apologise for that though," Harry added, slumping in his chair.

"After she called him creepy, mate. Not on really, is it?" Tim stated, swirling his pint.

"Just words," Simon grunted, shrugging his shoulders.

"What about dissing our main man Max? She wasn't even there! Max is mint, mate! Proper legend!" Jester slammed his fist on the wooden table below.

Harry drummed his fingers on the wooden table, looking for a tie to loosen, but absent once more.

"She's enthusiastic about this hobby, that's for sure."

Tim and Jester grinned at one another, as Simon fought the urge to doze off.

"Enthusiastic about something, Harold," Tim smirked. "She's invited you over to her flat to check out her outfit, mate."

Jester's eyes widened, lighting up with mischief. "Hah! 'Oh Harry, help me with my medieval corset, is this more period-appropriate on me or on your bedroom floor?'"

Simon stopped himself smacking Jester's arm, instead laughing heartily, Tim resisting the urge to join.

"Seriously though—Harry bruv, proper little penis fly trap you got there mate. Watch yourself!"

Tim was now laughing furiously, bashing his fist on the table, Simon glaring deeply at Jester.

"Really though, Harold," Tim began, calming his breath, "she's so obviously into you, mate. You need to let her down easy, if you aren't having a crack at it."

"It's already been made clear between us, Timothy. I'm her boss, and almost twice her age. We both know that—end of story. But she's lonely, and we're her group now too."

Harry glared, Tim and Jester cackling away. At least Simon had some decorum.

Chapter 21

Harry pulled on his tunic and tied his woven belt around his waist, handmade leather shoes slipped onto his feet like gloves. If they were attending a medieval market, he intended to look the part. Had taken all of his willpower to not throw the blasted phone out the window first, however. Bloody Barbie Girl.

A sharp tapping at the door startled Harry as he fumbled with an egg. Through the window, he spotted a familiar figure bouncing on his doorstep.

"Harry, bruv! Open up, it's bloody freezing out here!"

Harry opened the door to find Jester grinning widely, dressed in what appeared to be a jester's outfit—complete with bells on his cap that jingled with every little bounce.

Harry grinned from ear to ear. "Oh Jester, you look fantastic. A new addition to your medieval collection?"

"Yes mate! Medieval market, innit. Gotta look the part. I'm buzzing, I want me some mead and a mutton chop. Feel better if the big guy was with us though."

"You just want him to buy your lunch," Harry smirked, closing the door behind Jester.

"Come on mate, give us a Pepsi. I know you keep a stash for my visits. Not that I do—sorry, bruv."

Harry shrugged, smiling warmly at Jester, pulling a can from the fridge. It was moist and biting cold to the touch.

"Not exactly a forge's furnace out there today, Jester—you sure you wouldn't rather have a coffee?"

Jester's mind was already made up, the harsh click and satisfying hiss of the can declared it.

"Aw man, I remember that," Jester began, gesturing towards a photo of the group at Castle Rising on the wall. "Simpler times."

"Won't be long and we'll be back there again. Olivia in tow this time, perhaps."

Jester shrugged, before Harry continued.

"Well, the others should be here soon—oh bugger!"

Smoke began to trickle from the toaster, the smell of charred carbon tickling their nostrils as Harry ejected the toast.

"Ahhh! Nice one, mate! Max would be proud!" Jester roared, before chugging his can and crushing it with his hand.

A car door slammed outside. Through the window Harry could see his brother approach, Olivia adjusting something in the passenger seat.

Tim opened the door announcing "Knock knock! Morning, Harold. Ready for—bloody hell, what are you wearing, Jester?"

"Medieval market, innit? Gotta commit to the bit!" he replied, jingling the little bells on his head.

"Right, well, come meet our resident costume expert then."

They stepped outside where Olivia was climbing out of the passenger seat. She wore a deep crimson dress with golden embroidery that hugged her figure before flowing into a full skirt. The neckline was flattering, with delicate lacework that drew the eye. A leather corset cinched her waist, and her hair was braided with small wildflowers woven through it. The outfit was undeniably beautiful and historically accurate.

"What do you think, Harry?" she asked, doing a small twirl that made the skirt flare. "I stayed up until midnight getting the details right."

Job to stay professional, all that on display.

"Authentic. It's lovely, Olivia."

"I wanted everything to be perfect for today."

Jester's bells jingled as he mimicked his left hand clamping down hard on his right index finger.

"Right then," Tim said loudly as he grinned at Jester's antics, "shall we get moving? There's a long drive ahead and Jester's already moaning about being hungry."

"I haven't even started complaining yet!" Jester protested, climbing into the back seat.

Olivia hurriedly hopped into the front seat, adjusting her corset once more, admiring her handiwork in the mirror.

Harry fumbled with his key, hands shaking, as he aimed for the starter motor. Not even slightly distracting, that.

"Right then, belts on, ready to roll?"

"Crack on, mate," Tim said from the back. "Long drive ahead of us."

Harry caught a glimpse of Tim and Jester tapping away on their phones, presumably texting one another based on their giggles and guffaws.

"Something to share with the rest of the class?" Harry asked.

"Just showing my main man here a funny video about a Venus flytrap, bruv. Funny stuff, but you wouldn't get it."

Tim started cackling in the back, Harry gripping the wheel tightly, leather creaking under his knuckles.

"I'm really excited for today, Harry," Olivia began. "You can meet Master Preston and the others."

"Others?" Harry enquired.

"There's a whole bunch of vendors! I've been here a number of times over the years. Who knew we had the same hobby?"

Tim and Jester grinned at each other in the back, Jester jingling his bells.

"Seems like you knew, Olly, based on that sword you bought him. Quite a bit of kit that, mate," Tim said from the back.

"Oh, thank you! I was lucky, I got a really good deal. Well, it was worth every penny—Harry finally shut you up with it, didn't he?"

Jester's bells jingled some more as he began giggling in the back. "Sorry, bruv, she got you there. Harry kicked your arse, innit!"

Tim rolled his eyes, Harry staring intently at the road ahead, focusing on the hum of the tyres.

Nearly three hours of jests, jabs, and jingles and the bunch arrived at the medieval market in Coventry.

The crowd was immense, markets and stalls abound, people both in and out of medieval attire. All were welcome, whether in garb or otherwise.

Olivia hopped out of the car, once more giving a twirl, noticing Harry looking her way.

"Right then, boys. Let's take a look around."

Olivia skipped happily along next to Harry, Jester and Tim a short distance behind.

Harry's eye was caught by a leatherworking stall, run by a striking woman. A redhead, around thirty, wearing a piece of her handiwork—a hand-crafted leather corset. She leaned on the counter, leather creaking slightly.

Before he could consider, Harry blurted, "What a fabulous corset! You look fantastic. Did you work this yourself? The stitching is flawless."

Her grin curved, slow and wicked. "Well, handsome, if it looks fantastic here, it'll look twice as fantastic back in my bedroom?"

Harry froze, mouth open but no words came out.

Jester howled, bells jingling away, "Harry, bruv! She's serving it up and you get stage fright!"

The redhead plucked a scrap of paper from the counter, jotting down her number. "Call me for a custom fitting sometime, handsome." Her voice was husky with amusement.

"Th-thanks," Harry mumbled, Olivia tugging gently at the sleeve of his tunic.

"Bloody hell, mate," Tim started as they walked away, "She's a bit forward. No subtlety there."

Olivia's voice was light, almost playful. "Shame she's a three-hour drive. Not too practical for a custom fitting." She smiled warmly, fidgeting with her own corset.

Jester snorted, bells jingling as he cackled. "The only thing she wants to fit, Olly, is Harry's nob in her gob!"

Tim and Jester high-fived, laughing like mad.

"Oh Olly, I'm glad you suggested we come here, mate. Priceless, priceless comedy. Besides, Harold might finally get his end away!"

Harry's face turned a bright crimson, the droning voices of market patrons surrounding him, hammering his ears.

Olivia glared at the Jester and the Joker, laughing away behind them.

"Can't you see Harry is uncomfortable? Calm down. Let's go get you a drink, Harry."

Olivia led them towards a stall serving roasted legs of meat, honey mead, and Madeira cake. Jester wasted no time, purloining Harry's wallet from his pocket and getting to work.

"Hey! Jester that's—oh, what's the point."

Harry sat on a bench, closing his eyes for a moment, hands placed flat against the wood below.

Tim sat next to him, arm around his shoulder, Olivia off to scold Jester.

"Bit hectic in here, isn't it, mate? Want to head outside, find that forge building in a bit?"

Harry smiled, hand on top of his brother's. "That sounds good. I'll get my wallet back from the buffoon and we'll go take a look."

Suddenly, they were both startled by Olivia slapping Jester across the face, storming off as his bells jingled.

"Shit, Harold. What the hell? Right, you go after Olly, I'll talk to this joker."

Harry rushed to his feet, bobbing and weaving past patrons to find Olivia, quietly sobbing on a bench outside.

"Ah, there you are. You OK? What happened?"

Olivia brushed her eyes, straightening her corset. She re-affixed her smile, gazing over at Harry, twinkle in her eyes.

"Sorry, I didn't mean to lash out. He was cruel. He's been a buffoon all day."

Harry gently sat beside Olivia, placing a hand on her shoulder. She ignored it, hugging him tightly, crying a little more.

Harry patted her shoulder, looking for a tie to loosen, finding only the heat of the collar on his tunic.

"What was the disagreement about?" Harry pressed. He certainly didn't miss this kind of barely post-teens drama, Jester and Olivia being a similar age.

"I went to get your wallet back, Harry. I told him to get a job, get his own money. He made a vile remark about my job being your wench! Who does he think he is?"

Harry sighed, patting her on the back a little more, then pulling away to stand—offering her a hand.

"Kind of you to be so protective, but don't worry—I'll deal with Jester. Come on. Let's get you two to kiss and make up."

Olivia scowled, nearly visibly retching.

"Not literally!" Harry added.

They shared a brief moment of sorely needed laughter. Moments later, she bounced to her feet, happy little claps as she followed Harry back inside.

They brushed past the droning crowd, back to the food court where Tim and Jester had found a quieter corner.

"Harold, I've spoken to Jester. He's got something to say."

Jester looked up at Olivia, glaring a little, forcing a smile. "Olly, I'm sorry. I shouldn't have called you that. But you shouldn't mock my unemployment like that. I'm going through a hard time, OK?"

Harry smiled, nodding gently. The group turned to Olivia, all eyes on her.

There was a pause as she stared through Jester. Moments more passed, the awkwardness turning to tension. Finally, she smiled, and spoke.

"That's OK. I'm going through a lot too. I'm sorry I slapped you. Friends?"

Jester stood, bells jingling in tune. "We cool, Olly. But we ain't friends."

Harry frowned, as Tim and he looked at each other, wearing the same expression on their faces.

"Feels a little like babysitting medieval toddlers, mate," Tim began. "Kinda wish the big man was here now. He'd have sorted this out with one slap to Jester's arm."

Tim and Harry giggled to each other, Jester scowling.

"Let's go meet Preston! It's getting late. You're going to love him, Harry!" Olivia announced, gently tugging at the sleeve of his tunic.

Bobbing and weaving through the now dwindling crowd, they found their way out to the nearby shack, owned by forgemaster Preston.

He was staggeringly tall, muscular, not a hair on his head, face, or exposed upper body. Harry began to wonder if being shirtless was a requirement of the job.

"Ah, Olivia, my darling. Good to see you. And this fine young man must be Harry, right? I love the Jester costume!"

Jester howled. "Bruv, you just called me an old man! That's Harry." He gestured towards Harry, jingling the bells on his hat.

"Hah! Well, lovely to meet you, not quite so young man. I hope the longsword served you well. This little lady is a fierce negotiator—a bargain for her, but I just couldn't resist her charm—you know what I mean?"

Harry couldn't honestly say he did. Kind, thoughtful, intelligent—but never really felt charmed.

"A pleasure, Master Preston," Harry said, his gaze meeting a Viking broadsword hanging on the wall. Every bit the quality of the one Tim had bought him, with ornate, careful engravings on the side—even the scabbard.

"How much for that?" he stated plainly.

Before Preston could answer, Olivia interjected. "Isn't it a little short for you, Harry? Your longsword not suited to you?"

Harry shook his head. "It isn't that—I'd like a variety of weapons."

"Well!" Preston boomed over them both. "I've spears, axes, all manner of fine weapons. That one usually carries a stamp of £300. But I can already feel the glare of this little darling, pushing that down to £250 for yourself, Harry."

Olivia crossed her arms across her chest. "It's a little steep, even for your work, Pres. You sure about this, Harry?"

Harry was. He handed his card to Preston as he fetched the sword from the wall, presenting it to Harry—wrapping the hilt in cloth, forming a peace bonding.

"Sick, bruv! That's gonna look epic at the castle!" Jester jingled with joy.

Olivia stood close to Harry, admiring his new blade. "Suits you, dar—ha—choo!"

Harry glanced at her. "You alright, Olivia?"

"Sorry! Sneezed. Suits you, Harry!" She beamed brightly.

Olivia grinned, tugging at Harry's sleeve once more. "Well, thanks, Pres. See you again in another few months. Be well."

"And yourself! A true pleasure, gents. Take good care now. God bless."

Harry also had to wonder if godliness was a job requirement for blacksmithing, too.

"Man, I wish Si was here. He'd love the smithy here too. Though I gotta admit he did have some chemistry with that Max."

Jester sighed, jingling his hat.

"Well, my new broadsword is beautiful. Thanks for bringing us here, Olivia. Perhaps Preston is the master after all," Harry said as they ambled back towards the car.

"See, Harry! I know my stuff. I'll always look out for you," Olivia beamed, hooking her arm through Harry's.

"Now don't be so quick to side with Olly, Harold. You haven't seen Max's finished work yet," Tim interjected.

"Why don't you stick to selling cars, Tim? Harry knows quality medieval work when he sees it," Olivia responded snarkily.

Jester and Tim turned to face each other, making a mocking gesture—met with a glare by Olivia.

Harry unlinked arms, gently patting her forearm. "Thanks, Olivia, I'm fine. Right then, where to next? I've had enough of the market," he said.

"Harry, bruv, take us drive-thru! I want a cheeseburger," Jester fluttered his eyelids at Harry, grinning widely and jingling his hat.

Harry chuckled, almost dropping his new blade. "All right, all right. I can't resist your boyish charm."

"He's not your piggy bank, Jester," Olivia scowled. "You need to work for your own money."

Harry coughed, the air feeling thick, as Jester furiously jiggled his hat near Olivia.

"Ah, don't worry, Jester mate. I'll teach ya how to sell cars. Easy," Tim said.

"Can ya teach me how to sell Olly a sense of humour, bruv?"

Tim and Jester both started howling again, as Harry clambered into the driver's seat. He couldn't bear the thought of three more hours of this on the drive home. For a brief moment, he was tempted to leave them there and go back for that custom fitting.

Chapter 22

"Cheeseburger for Jester, then. Anyone else still hungry?" Harry asked.

"Get us one too, mate," Tim said.

"Just the chicken salad for me, please, Harry! What are you having?"

"I could devour a fish burger, honestly."

Olivia brushed his arm. "Maybe you should join me in the salad, Harry?" she suggested, gently poking his tummy and grinning.

"You his mum or something, Olly? Chill out, innit!" Jester mocked from the back.

"Let the man get his burger, Olly. Been a long day, mate," Tim chimed in.

"Fish burger, two cheeseburgers, chicken salad please," Harry stated curtly at the speaker.

As they pulled forward to the payment window, Olivia fiddled with her corset. Harry caught her reflection in the wing mirror, her face speckled with sadness.

"Sorry, Harry," she said softly as they waited for their order. "I didn't mean to overstep. I just worry about you."

"It's all right, Olivia, I know you meant well—I know you've no malice," Harry stated plainly.

Harry grabbed the paper bag from the next window, handing out the food. Jester obliterated his with three bites, Tim taking his time and savouring the flavour.

"That new blade, Harry—tight, bruv. That Preston does some good work. I'm excited to see my daggers next Friday though," Jester chimed in from the back.

"I'm going to call him tomorrow, and see if we can collect them Wednesday instead. That way, we can try them out at swords," Harry said.

"That forge was sound, Harold, but Max is the legend. Besides, good as this Preston is, can't beat our own hand-forged steel."

"You've tasted defeat at the hands of Preston's superior work, Tim," Olivia remarked.

"They both have their merits. My new blades are gorgeous, but I can't wait for my hand-forged short sword either. Like Tim said, we put our blood, sweat and tears into those."

Tim smirked as he polished off his burger. "So, Harry—you going to call that redhead? She's gagging for it, mate."

Harry flushed. "Timothy!"

"Not every day you get offered a custom fitting, bruv," Jester cackled, bells jingling.

Harry exhaled, forcing a half-smile. "Three-hour drive, isn't it? Hardly worth chasing."

In the wing mirror, he caught Olivia's reflection—her smile soft, her eyes shining just a little too brightly. She twisted the ribbon of her corset between her fingers, saying nothing.

As they drove home through the countryside, Olivia pointed out various historical landmarks with keen enthusiasm, a smile on her face.

"Olly, mate," Tim began, "how do you know all this stuff?"

"I spent a lot of my childhood learning. On the computer, in the library, that sort of thing."

"Sounds lonely," Tim replied.

"Foster system. Guest in every home I stayed in, always temporary. I found my own meaning in learning new things, I suppose. Books don't push me in the dirt, or mock me for my lack of parents, or send me away to another home."

The mood in the car shifted, a sombre silence settling in.

"Well, brothers in steel can make room for a little sister, right, mate?" Tim said softly, glancing at Jester.

Jester shrugged, bells jingling a little with the movement.

"Even if you do try to make Harold eat rabbit food."

Olivia laughed hard, snorting a little. "Right, I think I have been a bit food police lately. Sorry, Harry!"

Harry chuckled, smiling warmly. "Kind of you to care—but I'm getting my cinnamon swirls back."

Olivia mocked a little salute to him, the boys in the back laughing as Harry focused on the road.

The mood for the rest of the ride back lightened, soon the familiar sight of the sea declaring them home.

"Right then, best be getting off. Yvette will kill me if I don't get back soon to help with the boys. Jester, Olly, need rides home?"

Jester shook his head, bells jingling. "No way, bruv, I'm walking. I wanna turn some heads with my jinglies!"

"What if we all stay with Harry for dinner? What do you think?" Olivia asked, happy little claps at the thought.

Harry tugged at the neck of his tunic. "Sorry, not up for that. I'll see you first thing at work tomorrow."

Olivia frowned a little. "I understand, you need space. Well, I had a lovely time, Harry!" Olivia said, giving his arm a squeeze as she climbed into Tim's car.

Harry watched them drive away, embracing the cold, salt sea air for a moment before heading back inside.

After a roller-coaster of a day, Harry was glad to be home—now out of garb, crawling into bed and snuggling up with Mr Snuffles.

"That was quite a day, Mr Snuffles. A bit more dramatic than I was expecting," Harry whispered. "But at least it's over now."

Mr Snuffles didn't reply. He never did, of course, being a stuffed rabbit—but he sure was a great listener.

Chapter 23

"Morning, Harry!" Olivia beamed as he strutted through the front door of the office.

"Good morning! Let's have a great day today, after the action-packed weekend. What's on for today, then?" Harry asked, rubbing his tired eyes.

"Hope you had a lovely evening after we went home? Your first client, let's see—James Moore, school teacher, 29. A romance scam, agreed to transcription. I'll send him in when he gets here."

Harry nodded, pushing open the door to his office.

"Oh Harry! Just you wait until lunch. I have a surprise for you!" Olivia beamed as he walked through.

Harry was greeted by the familiar sugary sweet scent of cinnamon once more. He scurried to his desk, turned on his computer and ravenously obliterated a cinnamon swirl. No savouring, just crammed it into his mouth like the first food he'd eaten in days.

Moments later, his door creaked open, a tall and balding man stepping through. His posture was slumped and meek.

"Welcome, Mr Moore. Harry Maxwell, Harry is fine. Just double-checking, you're all right with transcription? Accessible only to myself and my secretary, and stored securely."

"Yeah, I do remember agreeing to that. If my notes can help other victims, please by all means. James is fine."

He scratched the back of his hand whilst staring forlornly at the pastries on the table. His gaunt appearance had Harry wondering if he'd eaten in a while.

"Help yourself, James. In your own time, tell me, what happened?"

James sat on the corner of the sofa.

"I met Amber on a dating app. I'd decided to get myself out there again, it being over a year since my divorce, house seeming a little too quiet with just myself and my teenage daughter at home."

Harry casually helped himself to another cinnamon swirl, gently nodding as he spoke.

"Well, she just seemed so interested in me. Always asked me how my day was, seemed positive about my hobbies, just generally really sweet and kind. She suggested we move over to WhatsApp, as things could start looking more intimate there."

James sighed heavily, head in hands.

"She started sending me these gorgeous pictures of herself, in lingerie, leaving little to my imagination. I was... I was enthralled, swept up by it all. I felt like a teenager again."

He paused a moment, seconds stretching.

"I'm so stupid. I didn't even think to call her, or see her, or... anything, really, before I...before I... reciprocated. I was lonely, and she used that."

Lonely and horny. Deadly combination.

"Was this where the threats came?" Harry probed gently.

"That's right. Said she had a picture of me naked, and it would be sent to everyone on my friends list on my social media if I didn't pay. They had me send bank transfers to some strange man I can't even pronounce the name of. They just kept asking for more money."

"I see. Well, firstly, James, I'm sorry to hear what happened—please don't blame yourself. They weaponised your loneliness against you in a profound and personal way. How much did you lose?"

James sighed. "£8,500. My entire savings. But it wasn't even really the money—they sent my photo anyway, when the money dried up."

His voice cracked, audibly raising an octave.

"Bunch of my Facebook friends saw it, including my parents—and my teenage daughter, for Christ's sake. She can't even look me in the eye—it hasn't reached school yet, but if it does, I could be in serious jeopardy."

Harry loosened his tie, choking once more.

"I'll take your case, if you like, see if we can help with the money. Standard five per cent recovery fee. When it came to the scammer's profile, how did you verify them?"

James scratched his head. "Well... I'll be honest, I was just taken in by how pretty she was. I googled the name, and it seemed like a real person."

Harry sat up, placing his palms against the desk. "I'll show you how to reverse image search, so you can verify who you're talking to. Scammers will often take photographs of models and influencers, using them as their own. You happy to show me the scammer's profile, if you still have it?"

James nodded, bringing it up on his phone and making his way over to Harry.

"Here, take a look. Your scammer's profile links to a lingerie model on a women's clothing website. Not famous, so not an instant red flag for you, but this is a way you can verify. Of course, meeting is the best way to know for sure, or at the very least a video call."

James shuffled back over to his seat. "I appreciate you showing me that. I really do feel like a fool now, though—what do I do?"

Harry looked over at his bookshelf.

"You rebuild. Talk it through with your daughter, James. Use it—tell her the dangers of meeting people online, and use it as a reason to reinforce the positive relationships in your life."

Harry paused a beat, sipping water.

"If you need to talk more, Olivia out front will book you in."

James rose to his feet, offering Harry a forced smile as he shuffled out of the office.

Lunchtime soon rolled around, the scent of strawberries competing with sugary cinnamon as Olivia emerged through his office door, bouncing happily on the spot.

"Harry! You ready for your surprise?"

Raven finally came with that winning lottery ticket?

Harry loosened his tie. "Of course, Olivia."

Olivia skipped out of the office and came back in with a plastic carrier bag. The smell was unmistakable—it was a Chinese takeaway.

"Oh! Fantastic!" Harry blurted, practically hovering out of his chair towards Olivia and the feast she'd offered.

Harry didn't know where to begin, eyes darting from one dish to the next, feeling like a kid in a candy shop. Egg fried rice, lemon chicken, fried noodles, even the spring rolls he'd been craving.

No words were exchanged, just satisfied, happy looks between the two of them as they feasted away.

Harry patted his belly, sighing deeply, slumping back in his chair.

"Oh dear. Are you trying to set me up for some bad news, Olivia? You've found a new job, is that it?"

Olivia giggled, shaking her head furiously. "I'll never leave you, Harry. Not ever. No bad news! Oh... except your next client is another whiskey barrel scam."

Harry narrowed his gaze, sitting upright in his chair. As he and Olivia exchanged glances, they both burst out laughing.

"Well, at least I'm ready for it now on a nice full stomach. We'll have to train extra hard at swords this week to work off this little feast. Right then, send in the next victim on the whiskey-go-round when they get here, please."

Olivia curtsied. "Will do, m'lord. Oh, by the way, I called your blacksmith for you. You can pick your weapons up Wednesday evening. I asked him very nicely, so they'd be ready in time for swords this week! Not bad for your own personal wench, hey Harry?"

They laughed together again, and Harry gave her a thumbs up as he slumped back in his chair once more, arms behind his head, relaxing.

Chapter 24

"Good work today, Olivia. Are you heading home now?" Harry said, closing his office door, Wednesday's trials complete.

"Not yet, Harry. Still working on my course. Don't forget to go pick up your weapons!"

Harry raised a finger, fumbling in his pocket for his phone.

"Brothers in steel, I'm off to Spalding to get our handcrafted blades! Want in?"

"Sold, bruv. But you're buying me a cheeseburger." Harry rolled his eyes at Jester's reply.

"Sure," Simon sent simply.

> *"No can do, Harold. Yvette's off out tonight, so I'm watching these two little terrors. Only fair though, since we got swords tomorrow, isn't it. Keep my blade safe for me, mate. Love ya boys."*

Harry smiled, waving to Olivia as he left the office and approached his car.

Once home, he hurriedly tore off his suit, eager to hop into jeans and a T-shirt—before Simon pulled up in his van, Jester in tow.

"Yo, Harry! Burning daylight, bruv. Let's go."

The three of them hopped into his car, Simon and Jester in the back. Harry felt a little like a chauffeur without someone up front.

Harry's phone buzzed in his pocket.

"Harry, did you read my latest paper about financial incentives for third-world governments to disassemble scam compounds? Think of the impact on human lives. I look forward to our video call on Friday, darling. Harriet x"

Jester tapped Harry on the shoulder. "Harry, text that leather bird later, innit. We gotta go!"

Harry rolled his eyes, slipping his phone back into his pocket. They set out once more to Lincolnshire, eager to behold the gleaming majesty of their hand-forged blades.

"So Harry, you texting her or not? She was well up for it. It ain't a short drive, but when's the last time you even shagged, bruv?"

Simon chuckled deeply from his seat, offering a fist for Jester to bump.

Harry gripped the wheel tighter, considering his reply.

"It was professional interest in her craftsmanship," he protested. "She was a master at her craft. I could see that."

"You could see a lot more than that when she leant over the counter, bruv!" Jester cackled. "She was serving it up on a silver platter and you went all deer in the headlights. Simon, back me up here."

"Absent!" Simon grunted with amusement.

Harry slapped his steering wheel. "Don't be silly. Besides, I'm sort of talking with this professor at the moment—she's intellectually stimulating."

"Oh yeah?" Jester perked up immediately, leaning forward between the front seats. "Who's this then? Don't tell me it's that dating app again. Christ, Harry, you've had more failed dates than I've had cheeseburgers!"

"It's not like that. Her name's Harriet. She's a doctor of psychology at the University of East Anglia. We've been talking for weeks now."

Jester's eyebrows shot up. "Talking? What kind of talking? Please tell me you've at least seen this bird naked, Harry."

"Jester!" Harry gripped the steering wheel tighter. "It's not about that. We connect intellectually. She understands my work. We have deep conversations about psychology, human behaviour, the nature of—"

"Boring!" Jester interrupted with exaggerated snoring sounds. "Simon, can you believe this? Our Harry's found himself a proper swot. Bet she wears glasses and everything."

Simon's chuckle turned into something approaching a laugh. "Careful," he rumbled.

"Careful of what?" Harry asked, glancing in the rear-view mirror.

"Smart women," Simon elaborated with unusual verbosity.

"See? Even the big man knows what's what," Jester said, settling back into his seat. "So have you actually met this brainiac bird then, or is this another one of your imaginary girlfriends?"

Harry's grip on the wheel tightened further, knuckles turning white. "We're meeting soon. We've had phone calls, and we're planning a video call this Friday actually."

"Video call?" Jester's voice rose an octave in disbelief. "Mate, you've been talking to someone for weeks and you've never even seen them properly? Harry, bruv, that's mental! Could be a bloke in a wig for all you know!"

"She's not a man in a wig," Harry said firmly. "Her profile is verified, she works at a legitimate university, she's published academic papers that I've read. She's intelligent, thoughtful, and she actually appreciates intellectual discourse."

"Right, right," Jester said, nodding sagely. "And I'm sure her intellectual discourse is proper stimulating and all that. But has she got nice tits?"

"Jester!"

"What? It's a valid question! Look, Harry mate, I get it. You want someone who can chat about all your psychology bollocks—but you're a man, yeah? With man needs. When's the last time you got your end away? Come on bruv, answer me already."

Harry felt his face burning now. "That's really not—"

"Ages, innit?" Jester continued relentlessly. "I can tell just by looking at you. You're all wound up like a spring, bruv. Proper tense, you are. What you need is that leather bird from the market. Guaranteed she'd sort you right out, no messing about with no intellectual discourse. Go get that custom fitting, innit!"

Simon coughed through continued cackles, grinning from ear to ear.

"Look," Harry said, trying to maintain some dignity, "physical attraction isn't everything. Harriet and I are building something deeper than that. We understand each other on a psychological level."

"Psychological level," Jester repeated mockingly. "Harry, mate, you can't shag a *psychological level*. Give that big-titted redhead a call, bruv. Go get it!"

Despite himself, Harry found himself grinning. "You're impossible."

"I'm realistic, bruv. You spend all day dealing with nutters and scammers, then you go home to your empty house and text some bird you've never met about intellectual discourse. That ain't on, mate."

"It's not an empty house," Harry protested weakly.

"My Pepsi in the fridge don't count as companions, bruv."

"I have a stuffed rabbit, actually. Mr Snuffles."

Jester dissolved into laughter. "Mr Snuffles! Oh, that's brilliant. Simon, did you hear that? Our Harry's got a stuffed rabbit called Mr Snuffles!"

Even Simon was openly chuckling now, his massive frame shaking with mirth.

"It's not funny," Harry said, but he was fighting back a smile himself. "He's... comforting."

"I bet he is, bruv. I bet he gives proper good intellectual discourse too."

The drive continued in relative silence, Jester flicking away on his phone with Simon staring out of the window, watching the fields go by.

"Seriously though, Harry," Jester said eventually, his tone slightly more serious. "This Harriet bird. You sure she's legit? I mean, no offence, but you counsel people who get scammed for a living, bruv. Don't that make you a bit paranoid?"

Harry considered this. "I've verified her profile. She's published academic work that I've read. Her university email address is legitimate. We've had extensive conversations about psychological theory that demonstrate genuine expertise. This is no scammer. Or if it is, it might actually be the Nigerian Prince."

"But you've never met her you said?"

"Not yet. We've a video call on Friday night, though, and we'll set up a date after that."

"Make it happen, Harry. If she won't meet, or makes excuses, that's a big red flag, innit?"

"She's not going to make excuses. She's genuinely busy though—her work is important."

"More important than meeting the man she's supposedly into, bruv?"

"It's not... we're not..." Harry trailed off, realising he wasn't entirely sure what he and Harriet were to each other.

"See?" Jester pounced. "You don't even know what you are to her. I may be unemployed and living in a shithole, but even I know that proper relationships involve actually being in the same room as each other occasionally."

Simon shifted in his seat. "True," he said simply.

"Exactly! Thank you, Simon. Look, Harry, I'm not trying to piss on your parade, but you're being a mug. This bird's stringing you along with fancy words and academic bollocks while you're sat at home every night texting her like some lovesick teenager."

He wanted to argue, but simply couldn't.

"Maybe you're right," he admitted quietly. "I fully intend to push for us to meet soon."

"Or," Jester said with renewed enthusiasm, "you could text that leather bird right now. I bet she'd meet you tonight if you asked. Proper woman, that one. None of this intellectual discourse bollocks."

"I'm not texting the leatherworker."

"Why not? What you got to lose? Your dignity? Hate to break it to you, bruv, but that ship sailed the moment you told us about Mr Snuffles."

"Right, well, we're nearly there now. Time to see if Max has turned our lumps of metal into real weapons or if we're going home with expensive paper weights."

They pulled into the familiar car park outside Max's forge, the building looking exactly as it had when they'd left their crude blades last weekend. Smoke still rose from the chimney, and the sound of hammering could be heard from within.

"In we go then," Harry said, switching off the engine. "Let's see what we've made."

The three of them climbed out of the car and approached the heavy wooden doors of the forge. The heat emanating from within warmed Harry's skin.

"Ah, the warriors return!" Max's booming voice greeted them as they stepped inside. "I had to work hard to have this ready in time. But I couldn't say no to that charming secretary of yours, Mr Maxwell."

"Harry can," Jester mocked under his breath to Simon.

The forge greeted them with the familiar scents of coal and heated metal.

"Let's see them then?" Jester asked eagerly.

"Over here," Max grinned, his massive frame silhouetted against the glow of the furnace. "Are you ready to see some fine steel?"

He gestured towards a wooden rack where four weapons hung in a neat row, each one gleaming despite the dim light of the forge. Even from a distance, Harry could see that they were beautiful—no longer the rough, crude shapes they had hammered out weeks earlier, but genuine forged steel.

"Bloody hell!" Jester exclaimed, gazing at the rack.

Simon simply nodded, but there was satisfaction in his expression as he surveyed their handiwork.

Harry approached his short sword slowly. The blade was perfect—straight and true, with a subtle fuller running down its centre. The crossguard was elegantly simple, and the grip had been wrapped in dark leather that felt comfortable in his hand as he gripped it tightly.

"This is incredible, Max," he said softly. "I can't believe we made this."

"You forged the blade," Max replied. "The steel remembers the hammer blows you gave it. Each weapon carries something of its maker's spirit."

Jester picked up his twin daggers, spinning them in his hands. They were smaller than the others' weapons but no less impressive—perfectly balanced and weighted to his needs.

Simon examined the claymore. The massive sword was even more impressive finished than it had been as raw steel. Nearly five feet of perfectly tempered metal, with an intricate crossguard that he could already see overpowering any foe foolish enough to be caught inside it.

"This is fine, fine work, big man," Max said, clapping Simon on the shoulder. "You've got the touch for this. Ever consider a career change?"

Simon just smiled and shook his head.

"And young Tim's sword is here too," Max continued, indicating a short sword similar to Harry's but with subtle differences in the pommel design. "Take it. You're all welcome back here any time."

By the time they loaded the swords and daggers carefully into Harry's car, darkness had fallen.

"C'mon, Harry," Jester said as they pulled out of the car park. "Cheeseburger time. And don't think I've forgotten about that leather bird either. You really should call her."

"I'm not calling her," Harry mumbled, conviction faltering.

As they drove through the darkening countryside towards their promised fast food stop, Harry noticed a "now recruiting" sign in the window.

Harry pulled into the drive-thru, the glow of the menu board illuminating their faces as Jester predictably ordered enough food for two people despite having no money to pay for it.

"Right then," Harry said as they got back on the road, the smell of cheeseburgers filling the car. "Those daggers of yours, Jester—genuinely impressive work. You put real effort into those."

"Cheers, bruv," Jester mumbled through a mouthful of burger.

"Makes me wonder," Harry continued, his tone casual but pointed, "why you can't channel that same focus and dedication into finding actual employment."

The car fell silent except for the hum of the tyres, driving through the flat fields towards Hunstanton.

Simon shifted slightly in his seat, glaring at Harry a little.

"What's that supposed to mean?" Jester asked, his voice losing its usual playful edge.

"Well, you clearly have the ability to work hard when you want to. Those daggers didn't forge themselves. You put in the work, some serious effort, and took pride in the craftsmanship—so why can't you manage the same with a job?"

"It's different, innit," Jester said defensively. "That was fun. Jobs are just soul-crushing bollocks."

"Oh, right. So the rest of us are just mugs then, are we? Tim selling cars, Simon fixing lorries, me counselling trauma victims—all soul-crushing bollocks?"

"That's not what I meant—"

"Because from where I'm sitting," Harry continued, pedal to the metal, "it looks like you want all the benefits of having money without any of the responsibility that comes with earning it. You spent the entire drive here taking the piss out of my love life, but at least I'm not sponging off my mates for dinner."

"Harry," Simon's voice carried a warning tone, his huge arms folded across his chest.

But Harry was on a roll now, months of frustration with Jester's constant mooching and mocking finally erupting.

"No, Simon, I think this needs saying. We all carry him—buy his food, pay for his drinks, even cover his

139

share of activities, like you paid for his daggers. And what do we get in return? Constant mockery and someone who thinks he's too good for honest work."

Jester had stopped eating, his burger forgotten in his lap. "You don't know what you're talking about, bruv."

"Don't I? Enlighten me then. What's so special about your situation that normal employment rules don't apply?"

"Enough!" Simon barked, the single word filling the car as heavily as his frame.

The silence was deafening. Harry glanced in the rear-view mirror and saw Jester staring out of the window, his usual cocky expression replaced by something much emptier.

"You really want to know?" Jester's voice was quieter now, lacking its usual bravado.

"Yes, actually. I do."

Jester was quiet for so long Harry began to think he wouldn't answer. When he finally spoke, his voice was barely above a whisper.

"I can't leave mum alone for eight hours at a time, bruv. She's not well."

Harry felt something cold settle in his stomach. "What do you mean, not well?"

"She's a junkie, all right?" The words came out in a rush. "Has been since dad fucked off when I was five. Some days she's fine, normal even. Other days I come home and find her passed out on the kitchen floor with a needle in her arm. So no, Harry, I can't just waltz off to some office job and pretend everything's fine."

The car fell into complete silence. Even the sound of the engine seemed muted.

"Christ, Jester," Harry said quietly. "I had no idea. I'm sorry."

"Course you didn't. Why would you? You've got your nice house and your important job and your psychological bloody discourse. Must be nice, living in a world where the biggest problem is whether some bird wants to meet you for coffee."

Harry looked for a tie to loosen, finding only a T-shirt. "I'm sorry. I shouldn't have—"

"Nah, you're right though, aren't you?" Jester's voice was bitter now. "I am a sponge. I do take the piss. Because this is the only normal I get. Few hours a week where I can pretend I'm just one of the lads instead of some loser whose biggest achievement is keeping his mum alive."

Simon spoke, his voice gentle. "Winner."

"Cheers, big man, but we both know that's complete and utter bollocks."

Harry pulled over into a lay-by, unable to concentrate on driving any more. He turned around to face Jester properly. "How long?" he asked.

"How long what?"

"How long have you been dealing with this alone?"

Jester shrugged. "Since I was a kid. Used to think it was normal, everyone's mums shooting up in the bathroom. Wasn't till I started school properly that I realised other families were different."

"And you've never sought help?"

"Who's gonna help? Social services? They'd just stick her in some programme she'd drop out of in a week. Police? They'd arrest her. Doctors? She won't go. So it's just me."

Harry stared at his friend—really looked at him for the first time in years. The constant jokes, the deflection, the way he always seemed to be performing rather than just being present. It all made sense now.

"The empty pockets," Harry said quietly.

"Yeah. Any money I do get goes on groceries or bills or... other stuff she needs. Can't exactly save up for a deposit on my own place when I'm buying needles to keep her from sharing dirty ones, can I?"

Simon reached over and put a massive hand on Jester's shoulder.

"You lot are the only thing that keeps me sane. Last thing I wanted was to turn sword practice into a bloody therapy session."

Harry felt ashamed of every time he'd rolled his eyes at Jester's requests for money, every joke he'd made about his employment status, every moment of irritation at his friend's apparent laziness. "I'm an idiot," he said finally.

"Yeah, you are," Jester agreed, but there was no malice in it. "But then again, so am I for thinking I could keep it hidden forever."

They sat in the lay-by for several more minutes, none of them quite sure what to say. Finally, Harry started the engine again. "We'll figure something out," he said.

"Like what?"

"I don't know yet. But we will. That's what brothers do, right?"

Jester managed a weak smile. "Brothers in steel, innit."

"Brothers in steel," Simon confirmed solemnly.

The rest of their journey was finished in solemn silence, the brothers of steel carrying far more than just their blades.

Chapter 25

Harry sat at the kitchen table, drumming away at it with his fingers. His phone buzzed.

"Harry, bruv, I'm gonna make you all proud. Just you watch. Jester."

Harry smiled, spinning the phone in his hands. Another text buzzed through:

"Harry darling, I hope you're ready for our video chat tomorrow. I'm sure it will be stimulating! Harriet x"

Harry slipped the phone back into his pocket, gazing at the photographs adorning the kitchen wall.

Harry nodded at the one of himself with his aunt. He'd been putting it off, as every time it got a little harder— but he knew what to do with his afternoon.

Harry hopped in his car and set off, gripping the wheel ever tighter the closer he got to his destination.

He pulled up in a spot and sighed, pit in his stomach.

The familiar smell of antiseptic and misery hit Harry as soon as he walked through the automatic doors of the nursing home. The cheerful receptionist looked up from her computer, offering the same practised smile she'd given him on every visit for the past three years.

"Here to see Caroline Brown?" she asked, already reaching for the visitor's log.

"That's right. Harry Maxwell, her nephew."

The woman's expression softened slightly. "She's having a bit of a hard time right now, Harry. Be prepared, OK?"

Harry nodded, signing his name with a hand that trembled slightly. He'd heard this warning before, but something in her voice made this one dig a little deeper.

He walked down the familiar corridor, past the communal lounge where elderly residents sat staring at a television none of them seemed to be watching. Harry paused outside her door, steeling himself before knocking gently.

"Aunt Caroline? It's me, Harry."

"Come in," came the voice from inside—still recognisably hers, though frailer than he remembered.

Harry pushed open the door to find Caroline sitting in her armchair by the window, dressed in the pink jumper he'd bought her last Christmas. For a moment, she looked exactly as he remembered her—the woman who'd taken him in after the crash and made him chicken noodle soup when he was sick.

"Hello," she said pleasantly, looking at him with polite curiosity. "Are you the new doctor then?"

"No, Caroline. It's Harry. Your nephew. I've come to visit, same as last month."

Her brow furrowed as she studied his face, searching for some recognition but finding none.

"I don't think we've met," she said carefully. "Are you sure you have the right room?"

"It's me," Harry said, moving closer. "Harry. You raised me after my parents died. Remember? You used to make me help with the laundry, despite my complaints."

Caroline's expression began to change, confusion giving way to fear.

"I don't know who you are," she said, her voice rising slightly. "I think you're confused, dear. My nephew died in a plane crash. Why would you bring that up?"

Tears welled within Harry's eyes.

"Caroline, please. Look at me properly. It's Harry. The plane crash was your sister, my mum. I'm your nephew, you took care of me when my parents, your sister, died."

But the fear in her eyes was growing, her hands gripping the arms of her chair.

"I don't know you," she repeated, more firmly now. "You're a strange man. A strange man here to rob me! Nurse!"

"Caroline—"

"Help!" she called out again, her voice cracking with panic. "Help me! There's a strange man in my room! He's a thief!"

Harry stepped back as if she'd struck him. "Caroline, please, it's me. Don't you remember? You said I reminded you of your father, a big golden heart just like him. Please, auntie. Please."

"Help!" she called again, louder this time. "Someone help me! I don't know this man!"

Footsteps hurried down the corridor. A nurse appeared in the doorway, taking in the scene quickly.

"What's happening here?" she asked, moving protectively towards Caroline.

"There's a stranger in my room," Caroline said, pointing at Harry with a shaking finger. "I don't know who he is. Make him go away. He's scaring me."

The nurse looked at Harry with a mixture of sympathy and authority. "Sir, I think it's best if you step outside for a moment."

"But I'm her nephew," Harry said desperately. "I visit every month or two. I'm listed as her next of kin."

"I understand," the nurse said gently, "but she's very distressed. I really think you should leave. I'm sorry."

Harry looked at Caroline, hoping for some flicker of recognition, some sign that the woman who'd raised him was still in there somewhere. Nothing. Bugger.

"I'm sorry," he whispered meekly.

He turned and walked out of the room, past the concerned nurse who was already comforting Caroline, past the other residents who'd emerged from their rooms to see what the commotion was about.

The receptionist looked up as he approached. "Mr Maxwell? Is everything all right?"

"She doesn't know me," Harry said, his voice coming out flat and hollow. "She thinks I'm a stranger."

"I'm so sorry. The progression can be very rapid. Would you like me to arrange for you to speak with one of our counsellors?"

Harry shook his head. He counselled people himself. He knew all about the stages of grief, about acceptance and letting go. None of that knowledge made this hurt any less.

He walked out into the car park, fumbling for his car keys with hands that wouldn't stop shaking. She was gone.

Not dead, which would have been kinder. Just replaced by a frightened stranger who looked exactly like her.

Harry sat in his car for a long time, staring at the building that now felt like a mausoleum.

His phone buzzed with messages, but he couldn't bring himself to look at them. He was supposed to go to sword practice tonight. He was supposed to be strong, dependable Harry who had his life together.

Instead, he was just a lost boy again, tears falling from his eyes on the drive home.

He mindlessly felt the click of the lock on his front door, marched upstairs and held on to Mr Snuffles for dear life.

Time passed. He wasn't sure how much of it, but it must have been hours. There was a knock at his front door, but he hadn't the will to move, much less answer it.

Still, he was startled upright when he heard the door open and someone stepped inside.

"Harold? You here? Been trying to reach you, mate!"

Oh. Right. Harry had given his spare key to his brother. That was a smart move, wasn't it.

"Christ, there you are, Harry. You had us worried, mate. What happened?"

Tim came and sat next to him on the bed, offering him a shoulder to steel himself on.

"Aunt Caroline. She's... Her dementia has advanced to the point she doesn't even recognise me, Tim."

Tim patted Harry on the back. "That sucks, mate. Must confess, I haven't seen her in years. I know you two were close since she took you in. Harold mate, you're not sitting here on your own. I'm taking you to swords. Not taking no for an answer."

"Tim, I really don't—"

"What did I just say, Harold? Get your arse up. Besides, you got my new short sword!"

Harry dared to crack a little smile, even a brief chuckle at that comment. Tim helped him to his feet and brought the kit to his car.

"You alone?" Harry asked, as Tim helped him to the car.

"Yes, mate. Olly let the others in. She insisted on coming with me, but I told her she had to stay there as the keyholder."

"Thank you."

The hum of the tyres gave Harry peace on their way to the church. Tim hadn't really said much, just left him alone to process.

They pulled up to the church, light of the moon cast over the car park.

"Come on, Harold. Switch that brain off for a couple of hours, and come bash a brute with a short sword."

Tim lugged Harry's kit bag over his shoulder, two orange blinks from the car as he locked it remotely.

The clanging of steel echoed through the hallowed halls as Jester danced daggers around Simon and his new claymore.

Olivia had neglected to bring her armour—she instead came in garb, wildflowers and all, sat on the pew fiddling with leather.

"Hi Harry!" she called out, setting her leatherworking tools aside and rushing over, hugging him tightly.

Any other night, this may have felt awkward. But tonight, Harry hugged her back as the scent of strawberry danced in his nose.

"Harold's having a bit of a tough time today, everyone," Tim began, the clanging of steel paused. "Aunt Caroline's dementia has progressed. She doesn't recognise him."

Jester hopped over, patting Harry on the shoulder. Simon too, giving Harry a great big awkward bear hug, nearly snapping his back—or so it felt.

"Steel, brother," Simon decreed.

"What he said, bruv. I'm sorry. Be strong, yeah? Come on then, get yourself suited up, Harry. I've been working on something you're gonna love."

Jester beckoned for him to follow, leading him to the front pew. He helped Harry affix his armour, thrusting his new short sword in his hand.

"Tim, get yours too. Si, come here, bruv. Right, right. Go with me here, boys. Castle this Saturday, we need some showy scenes, right? I'm not saying we fully choreograph them or whatever. But how about you two boys face off against Simon, like we said before?"

Simon stood sentinel, arms folded, grinning and nodding happily.

The two brothers turned to one another, mustering smiles. "Let's do it, Harold. The brothers versus the brute. It'll be a crowd favourite!"

Harry's smile widened, though it didn't dare spread to his eyes.

"Perhaps Harry should use his new longsword instead?" Olivia offered from the bench, back to fiddling with her leatherworking tools.

"Nah, Olly, it works better like this. Simon has the reach and the guard to take them both on if they're using shorter blades. We don't wanna muddy that," Jester stated, unusually plainly for him—not a jest or a jibe in sight.

Olivia shrugged, turning her attention back to her leather.

"Let's give it a go. Si, you got more reach on your zweihander, but a better guard on your claymore. What you think?"

Simon gripped the hilt of his claymore tightly, stepping into the designated arena.

"Well, that answers that one. Right, boys, get in there then. Tim, bruv, come at Si. Get a rhythm going. Then Harry steps in too. Let's see it. Lay on arms!"

Jester stepped back, giving them space to fight. Olivia placed her tools to the side, staring intently at Harry.

Harry and Tim spread out, flanking Simon on either side. The massive man stood relaxed in the centre, claymore held in a guard position, the blade's dull point resting against the stone floor.

"Come," Simon rumbled, lifting the heavy blade with surprising ease.

Tim moved first, circling to Simon's left while Harry approached from the right. Their short swords felt almost toy-like compared to the massive claymore, but they had speed and numbers on their side.

"Now, Harry!" Tim called out, lunging forward with a thrust towards Simon's midsection.

Harry mirrored the attack from the opposite angle, but Simon was ready. He pivoted smoothly, bringing the claymore up in a wide arc that caught both blades simultaneously, the clash of steel on steel ringing through the hallowed halls like a church bell.

The impact sent vibrations up Harry's arm, but he pressed forward, trying to get inside Simon's guard while the bigger man was committed to the parry. Tim had the same idea, both brothers converging on their friend.

But Simon stepped back, using his reach, and brought the claymore down in an arcing strike. Just like that, victory was his.

"Fight! Sorry, boys, Simon's just on another level. That was beautiful! Pure poetry. I'm getting emotional."

The four of them came together announcing "Brothers in steel!" proudly through the church.

Olivia rolled her eyes, then returned her attention to the leather.

Tim and Harry caught their breath, sat on a pew. "Jester's onto something here, Harold. If we can pull off a fight like that at the castle, we'll make the local paper!"

Hurt hadn't left, but he'd forgotten about it for a while.

"Let's pack up, boys. Harry, bruv, I want to thank you for that little talk we had. It means a lot. I've got a part-time job to look forward to now, just gotta review products. Bloody good pay."

Harry listened, but didn"t hear a word.

"Jester," Simon gestured, calling his friend to go, Jester bounding out the church after him.

"Right, Harold. Let's get you and Olly home then. I'm always a call away if you need me, mate."

The church fell dark, the ancient oak doors creaked shut, as the halls fell silent once more. *Thief!*

Chapter 26

The horrible, dreadful wailing of Barbie Girl just served to anger Harry today. He often wished there was a day every week where absolutely nothing was expected of you, not even breathing.

Sadly, frantic Friday was no such day. There would be clients, responsibilities, the world would keep turning.

Harry took solace in the fact that Auntie Caroline wasn't suffering, not really. She had no idea what she was going through. It was his shoulders that had to bear the burden.

He sighed, already longing for the day to be done. His phone buzzed with a text from Harriet.

> *"Harry darling, tonight's the night then. Hope you're as excited as me! Harriet x"*

He rolled his eyes—he really wasn't.

"Not in the mood," Harry tapped out, pausing above send. He sighed, deleted it and tried again.

> *"Harriet, I may need to cancel. I'm afraid I'm going through a lot, my aunt's dementia has progressed. Harry x"*

Moments later, a reply buzzed through.

> *"Oh Harry, I'm so sorry. I understand that loss just as much as you do—they are still there, but they*

also aren't. You look at them, knowing who they
are, but they don't see you. They never see you.
You may as well be invisible to them as they look
right through you. Well, I'll still be available to
call if you fancy it. Don't worry, I won't
psychoanalyse you! Harriet x"

Bit of an essay, but wanted him to feel better. He did manage a brief smile.

One warm, tight hug with Mr Snuffles, his fur soft against Harry's cheek, and he mustered the will to take on the day. Might be needing that whiskey after all.

"Good morning, Olivia," Harry stated as he walked meekly through the door.

"Good morning, Harry, hope you're OK?"

Harry shrugged, sighing a little. "I will be, thanks. I'll be in my office."

"OK, Harry! See you at lunch."

He creaked open his office door, clicking it shut behind him. Cinnamon swirls didn't seem so appealing today. The morning went by in a flash of whiskey barrels and fake celebrity endorsements.

Olivia pushed open the door as lunchtime arrived.

"Hi Harry!" Olivia beamed as she creaked open the office door, bearing a Tupperware.

"I made one of your favourites. Take a look!"

She cracked open the lid to reveal a cheesy, creamy macaroni cheese.

The moment was interrupted by a phone call, Harry gulping fast and fumbling for his phone.

"Jester?"

"Harry, bruv."

Jester didn't sound himself at all. Deflated, depressed, defeated.

"I—I think I been scammed, innit."

Harry sighed and loosened his tie. "Damn. I'm sorry. Come down, we can talk?"

"I'll be there."

The call ended with a click.

"Olivia, please cancel or rearrange my next appointment," Harry said, sighing as he slipped the phone back in his pocket.

"Are you sure, Harry? It was an investment scam, art-related. A lot of money."

Harry narrowed his gaze. "Of course. I need to help Jester. Thanks, Olivia."

Olivia shrugged. "I think it's the wrong call, Harry. But you're the boss!"

She offered a little curtsy and a grin as she headed back out to her desk.

Part-time job, review products, good pay—it had all been right there, had been so obvious.

Several minutes later, Harry was startled by a buzz from the intercom.

"Your next client is here, Harry, sending him in."

Seemed an odd way to describe Jester, as he meekly sauntered through the office door and slumped into the middle of the sofa.

Jester looked sad, sour—a complete juxtaposition to his usual irritating yet comedic self.

"Hi Jester."

Jester shook his head. "Harry. I didn't want to be here, but I need your help, and—well, it all happened so fast. Please, just don't judge me, as a friend and a... whatever you call yourself here, innit."

"Tell me what happened—in your own words, when you're ready."

Didn't need to ask. Pretty clear by now, but gave Jester a chance to talk it out.

"Well, that's exactly it, bruv. You've all been on my case lately about getting a job, and I see this advert. It was perfect. All I had to do was review products, and they pay me. You only work two hours a day, and it's ten times the money I get from benefits, so of course I was hooked. I tried to tell you about it last night at swords."

Employment scams. Some victims paid thousands to the schemes before the penny dropped, realising the payment they were apparently due was fabricated.

Harry sighed, solemnly nodding his head.

"Look, Harry, I'm not blaming you all for this. But I felt it was the right thing at the right time, you all pushing me to get back into work, innit. They took the scraps I'd saved for driving lessons. I'm screwed."

Jester fought back tears.

"I'm sorry I didn't hear you last night, Jester. You tried to tell me about this. I... I could have warned you," Harry lamented.

"Yeah, I guess it did sting a bit." Jester relaxed his shoulders and sat back into the sofa, staring at the bookcase.

"All that employment talk, your searches, probably steered that advert right to you with your browsing cookies. The right job on the right advert at the right time, straight after our talk. Perfect storm."

"Oh yeah. Those are the worst. You're right about it all. Was on my phone, just right there. It was so perfect, Harry. I don't know what to do, bruv."

"Don't lose hope, Jester. We'll try our best to help, no fees. I'm sorry."

Harry stood to shake his hand, no words spoken on Jester's exit.

Olivia slipped in and locked the door behind her.

"What happened, Harry? Is Jester all right?"

Harry kept his gaze on the desk. "Jester's all right. Sorry, Olivia—I didn't have his permission to transcribe this one. I can't share."

Her shoes scuffed the carpet as she shifted. "Harry, it's me. I'm his friend too. I'm part of the group. It wouldn't hurt to tell me."

Harry finally looked up. His arms folded across his chest, voice clipped, professional. "Ask Jester."

The air between them grew heavy. Olivia's smile vanished into a tight glare, but Harry didn't flinch.

She rolled her eyes, spun round and left the room.

The latch clicked. Harry exhaled hard.

He gazed off at the bookshelf, beyond ready to go home.

Chapter 27

Laptop open, Harry tested the video worked. Once satisfied, he slumped in his chair.

The video call notification chimed at exactly eight o'clock—Harriet was punctual this time, he'd give her that.

He clicked accept, and there she was. The face matched her photos perfectly—intelligent green eyes behind thick glasses, auburn hair pulled back in a practical ponytail, the kind of understated beauty that spoke of academics.

"Harry! How lovely to finally see you properly," Harriet said, her voice warm through the laptop speakers. "Can you see me properly? Feeling any better after yesterday?"

"Better, thank you. And thank you for understanding. I can see you just fine. I like your glasses, they're cute."

Harry gently bit his tongue.

"Of course, thank you handsome. Actually, your situation with Caroline inspired some thoughts on my latest research. I've been working on a paper about invisible caregivers—people who provide constant emotional support but receive no recognition for their efforts."

Harry leaned forward, intrigued despite his melancholy—the handsome comment hitting harder than expected. "Fascinating. What's your thesis?"

"Well, it started when I was observing patterns in my students, darling. So many people, particularly those in helping professions, develop what I'm calling 'recognition deficit disorder.' They become so accustomed to being overlooked that they stop expecting acknowledgment anywhere in their lives. Invisible, unsung heroes, if you will."

Harriet adjusted her glasses, settling into her chair.

"The most striking finding was how these individuals often experience a kind of emotional invisibility. They're providing care, offering support, sometimes literally keeping other people functional, but it's as if they don't exist to those they're helping."

Harry nodded slowly. "I see that with my clients sometimes. Once they've recovered, moved past their trauma, it's like our sessions never happened. They're grateful in the moment, but forget soon after."

"Exactly! And that creates this interesting psychological pattern. The caregiver begins to question their own value, their own visibility. They start seeking recognition in other places, often forming intense connections with people who do see them."

Something in her tone made Harry pause. "You sound like you have personal experience with this."

Harriet smiled, but there was something sad in her expression. "Don't we all, to some extent? I think anyone who chooses a helping profession has experienced being overlooked, undervalued. It's what draws us to want to help others."

"I hadn't thought of it that way."

"The research shows that these invisible caregivers often develop blind spots about recognition in their immediate environment. They're so focused on providing care that they miss when someone right in front of them is trying to offer the same support back."

"What do you mean?"

"Well, take your situation with Caroline. You've been visiting her, caring for her, but she can't see you anymore. That pain you're feeling—it's not just about her condition. It's about being invisible to someone you love. But I wonder... are there people in your life who do see you, who recognise what you do, but perhaps you don't notice because you're so used to being overlooked?"

Harry tapped his fingers against the desk. "I suppose I haven't really thought about it."

"The most interesting cases in my research were people who formed deep emotional connections through distant relationships—online friendships, professional correspondences, academic collaborations. They were starving for recognition, so when someone finally saw them, really saw them, the connection felt incredibly profound."

"That makes sense psychologically."

"But here's what I found troubling, Harry. Many of these subjects had people in their immediate circle who'd been providing emotional labor for them— colleagues who went above and beyond. But because these caregivers weren't asking for recognition explicitly, they remained invisible."

Was this a lecture or a date?

"I'm curious about your own experience," Harriet continued. "In your work, your personal life—do you ever feel like you're the one providing all the emotional support? Like people take your care for granted?"

"Sometimes. I think I follow your research interests now," he said slowly. "You're suggesting that helpers can be helped without realising it."

"Precisely. And sometimes the people offering that help are right there, in their daily lives, but they've become as invisible as the helpers themselves feel. It's a tragic cycle, really."

Harriet leaned forward slightly, her voice becoming softer as the blurred background flickered. "I hope you don't mind me saying this, Harry, but our conversations have made me wonder if you're experiencing some of this yourself. You speak so thoughtfully about caring for others, but when do you let others care for you?"

Harry felt heat rising in his cheeks. "I'm not sure I understand."

"Do you overlook the caregivers in your own life, Harry?"

A thoughtful but plainly stated question.

"I don't believe I do, to be honest. I take care of my friends and employee, as best I can."

There was a brief pause, Harriet grinning.

"You strike me as a decent and honourable man. I could easily find myself falling for a man like you, caring for a man like you. Perhaps we should meet, Harry?"

The embers of hope sparked to life in Harry's chest.

"Oh! Yes! I'm very much inclined to agree to that. Tonight?"

Harriet laughed, snorting a little. "Calm down, Romeo. How about at the weekend?"

Harry frowned. "Sorry, but I can't do this weekend. I'm at Castle Rising for a medieval event. But you could come?"

"Quaint. Sorry darling, not my cup of tea. How about next Friday, then? We could watch a film couldn't we, then discuss it over dinner after?"

Harry was practically bouncing. "It's a date! Next Friday it is, then."

"How lovely. Toodles, darling."

The call dropped, as Harry breathed deep, calming the pounding in his chest. Won't be needing those swimming trunks this time.

Chapter 28

The horrible wailing of the alarm assaulting his ears, Harry could practically feel the electricity in his nerves as he sprang out of bed and shut the bloody thing up.

Two impending events competed within him to lift his spirits—the Castle and the upcoming date night. He felt as if he were going to burst.

Harry rushed to get ready, barely feeling the cold, harsh water of the shower cascading against his tingling skin.

Still awake and alert, he double- and triple-checked his kit bag and garb, tunic and belt adorning him.

Straight out the door, barely before six in the morning, the sun daring to rise over the calming ocean waves on the horizon.

Harry finally pulled into the car park at Castle Rising. He was first to arrive, as he was every year—getting a jump on assembling the medieval-style tent he'd lugged in the boot.

The beams were built of solid oak, heavy yet durable, designed to outlast even him. It did seem impractical to take on this effort alone, first thing in the morning, when Simon would arrive an hour or so later—but it had become almost a ritual and a point of pride to Harry.

The sun peaked over the horizon, illuminating the glorious green fields of the castle grounds. The weathered castle stood proudly at their centre, as it had for centuries before.

Harry leaned back and relaxed in his camping chair, enjoying the birds as they began their morning mating calls. He was grateful he had the app to make those calls for him—imagining his throat would be rather hoarse by now.

Still, with a little luck, the cinema date next week could be the start of something special. No more expired subscriptions, awkward chemistry lectures, or stand-ups at the coffee shop.

Before long, Simon's van pulled in, Tim following shortly after. A few other re-enactors had begun to dribble in too, their own displays to arrange.

"Harold!" Tim called, as the brothers in steel lugged their kit over, Olivia skipping in tow. "Come give us a hand, mate."

Harry sprang up, yawning deep from his belly, and trotted over to grab a bag.

"Hi Harry!" Olivia beamed, wildflowers in her hair, dressed precisely as she had been at the medieval market—though her corset was noticeably different. "I've been teaching myself leatherworking amongst my other hobbies and studies. Do you like my corset?"

Harry smiled, tugging at the collar of his tunic. "Looks lovely, Olivia."

She bounced on the spot, happy little claps and all.

"Harry, bruv, stop staring at Olly's tits and help us already!" Jester jabbed.

He soon regretted it, Simon smacking him in the arm and scowling. Olivia blushed and giggled a little.

"Excuse me," Harry said, offering her a practised smile as he grabbed a beam from Jester.

Before long, both tents were set up, but Harry needed to address the elephant in the room.

"Right, how are you getting home tonight, Olivia?" Harry asked. "It isn't too far, I could probably run you back. Or Timothy?"

Olivia shook her head. "I wanted to come camp with the steel brothers, Harry! I'm sure there's room to squeeze me in somewhere. Can't I just cuddle up with you?"

Harry's eyes widened, chest tightening at the thought of her young, warm body pressed against his as strawberry scents lingered in his nose.

He quickly and furiously shook his head, tugging at his collar. "Not appropriate, I think," he stated, Simon nodding as he folded his arms, standing sentinel.

"Never mind that, Harold, we'll sort something out later. Right now, I've just seen the doughnut van pull up. Medieval or not, I'm getting me some fried fatty goodness for breakfast."

Back in a flash, Tim distributed doughnuts, Olivia kissing him on the cheek.

"Calm down love, Yvette'll kill me!" Tim said.

"Too late, Olly, he's hooked up, innit. Your boy Jester here on the other hand," Jester suggested, jingling his bells now he was happily back in his jester's outfit.

"Oh Jester, I'm sure you have enough to worry about right now without worrying about girls."

Jester frowned, the jingling of his bells falling silent. "Yeah, you're probably right," he stated plainly as Simon patted his shoulder.

"Damn, Harold, look over there!"

Tim pointed to another display group nearby, setting up their own tents and boundaries. It was clear where he was pointing—a huge, hulking giant of a man that dwarfed even Simon.

"Bloody hell!" Simon exclaimed, setting eyes on the huge man as he effortlessly lugged two kit bags over each shoulder.

Jester's bells jingled to life once more. "Boys. Brothers. Mates. This is happening. Simon versus Goliath. It's totally on, innit!"

Simon was grinning from ear to ear, his gaze fixed firmly on the giant.

"Well, you've planted the seed now, Jester. Simon's going to get his man today, I'm sure of that," Harry said, now sat back down enjoying the warmth of the sun mingling with the cool autumn breeze.

"Our own displays to think about first, boys. We'll go speak with them later, during a break. Crowds will be here soon—let's display the gear."

The brothers in steel got to work, display racks for weapons and armour showcasing their pieces. Harry added his longsword, short sword, and new broadsword to the rack as he looked forlornly over at his old Viking broadsword—now belonging to Olivia.

She proudly racked her entire set of ornate plate mail, front and centre, clapping happily when it was complete.

Patrons began arriving by the dozen, soon more than a hundred. A crowd was building fast. They were quickly surrounded by those in garb, and not, all welcome to attend.

Displays were set up all around them, from medieval crafts to feasts, others preparing for their own displays.

"Right then, lads—I feel it's time to armour up," Tim declared.

Jester was way ahead of him, out of the jester's costume and into his armour, already striking away at a pell with his twin daggers.

Moments later, their armour was secured, helms atop their heads.

Curious onlookers gathered around the barriers they'd set up, already whispers and murmurs amongst the quickly growing crowds.

Simon stood sentinel, claymore in hands, preparing to face the brothers both.

Jester abandoned his pell and stood ready to marshal.

"Lay on arms!" he roared, the clang of Simon's claymore meeting Tim's short sword crying out in the field around them.

It didn't have the same biblical echo as the hallowed halls of the church, but it drew the patrons nonetheless, murmurs and claps rising from the growing crowd.

Tim and Harry both attempted overhead blows, Simon catching them both on his blade, deflecting them sharply.

He swept his blade in a low arc, narrowly avoiding Harry's greaves, Tim blocking with a narrow drop.

The fight continued for some time, metal on metal, steel on steel. Simon parried an arm blow from Harry, catching him in his guard, overpowering and disarming him.

With Tim remaining, he soon fell to Simon's relentless, powerful blows.

"Fight!" Jester called, applause from the crowd as the three of them took a bow. It wasn't quite the feat of their trial at the church, but with the sun glaring in their eyes and them exposed to the crowd and the elements, they were not at their best.

Olivia stood at the boundary, ready to answer questions from onlookers.

"Why yes, the weapons are very sharp. One wrong move, and they'd take Sir Simon's head clean off!" Olivia giggled to herself, answering a horrified onlooker.

"Olivia," Simon said, shaking his head, but visibly smiling under his helm as the brothers chuckled.

"Olly, love, that was mean. But respect, respect," Jester said, patting her on the shoulder.

Tim and Harry placed their helms back on the racks, flopping into camping chairs, catching their breath respectively.

Moments later, Harry breathed deeply, watching more onlookers admire the racked weapons and armour. Olivia stood gracefully near her ornate plate mail, offering twirls and curtsies to passers-by, posing for the camera.

"I gotta admit, Harold, she's taken to this well. Bit more dramatic round here since she joined though. Maybe Jester was onto something with that no-dick-no-entry policy!"

Harry smacked Tim gently in the arm, clank of gauntlet against gauntlet, but both chuckling heartily.

"Yeah. She means well, though. I don't doubt that. And to be honest, she does a lot for me. She gives a lot of care, and I don't really see it. It's almost become second nature to me," Harry admitted.

"She's your secretary, Harold. She's supposed to care. You pay her to care," Tim retorted, sharp as a blade's edge.

They sat back in comfortable silence, whiling away the hours until the late afternoon struck. Jester and Simon had duelled once more, drawing a crowd themselves as Jester nimbly ran rings around his bear-like opponent. They were a crowd favourite.

Sensing a natural lull in the crowd, Simon beckoned for the others to follow, sheathed zweihander slung over his shoulder.

"Ahhh. I've been looking forward to this all day, bruv!" Jester announced, as the four of them left Olivia at their camp to meet the hulking brute and his crew.

"Well now," the giant man said, voice booming, instinctively lifting the barrier for Simon on their approach. "If ever I've seen a man who might match my power, it's you. Brutus of the Boston Blades. You?"

"Simon. Brothers in Steel!"

"Brothers in steel!" the other three echoed, Brutus grinning widely.

Simon clasped gauntlets with him and they shook, Brutus soon heading to his weapon rack, helm secured.

A crowd was already beginning to gather, phones held high, as Brutus retrieved a pair of claymores from their weapon rack, effortlessly spinning them in his huge hands. It was clear from the start this was a man of experience and power, and he wouldn't be going easy on Simon.

Simon's face was awash with glee, zweihander at the ready. The others watched in awe, not a word spoken between them. Even the crowd fell silent.

As the two brutes circled one another, a larger crowd naturally began to form and rather quickly, dozens of event patrons were now staring with phones held high. A real crackling energy of suspense permeated the air and audience both.

They kept circling one another as the crowd expanded, joined by Olivia and Yvette with the boys— their arrival noted by neither brother, nor Jester.

"Look at that crowd, big man. You ready?" Brutus said, spinning both his claymores skilfully still, the anticipation in the air about ready to burst.

Simon nodded. Brutus ruthlessly roared as he swept towards Simon, both claymores furiously trying to strike him. Simon skilfully caught both blades against his, as they grated against his edge—the clang heard across the field.

The crowd erupted into furious roars of joy, drawing more people still quickly around.

Simon brought his zweihander down on Brutus's head, but he crossed his claymores and caught it with ease. He pushed back, scraping metal on metal and staggering Simon, putting him off guard.

As good as Simon was, he couldn't deny Brutus was better—but he wasn't beaten, and wasn't going down without a fight—or a show.

The skilful exchange of furious sword blows continued for some time, until Brutus grew visibly tired. He was better, Simon knew, but he clearly lacked his stamina.

Harry cottoned on to this, too. All those giant muscles on Brutus were for show, probably hours in the gym, potentially even steroids in the arm. But Simon was a hard-working lorry mechanic, with the kind of natural strength and endurance that laborious work brings. Still, even amidst the spectacle of the duel, Caroline yelling "Thief!" pierced his mind.

Brutus began to struggle, flailing and missing his attacks. He tossed a claymore aside and wielded one with both hands—clearly not finished yet.

Simon grinned, baring his teeth beneath his helm. He was tired, too—but this was the fight of his life and he was relishing it.

They circled around each other a little more, Brutus panting heavily. He charged at Simon, sword overhead—a final gambit, going for the victory blow.

Simon was ready, though. The claymore clanged loudly against the guard rail of Simon's zweihander, echoes of furious metal screaming into the air around them. His sword caught, Simon skilfully twisted his zweihander and forcibly disarmed Brutus.

He looked at the discarded claymores, calmed himself and yelled "Yield!"

Simon and Brutus hugged one another, panting heavily. No words spoken, just mutual respect, bonds forged through steel and combat.

"That. Was. EPIC!" Jester roared, absolutely enthralled by the display.

He wasn't the only one. The immense crowd were completely taken aback by the furious display, cheering, roaring and applauding with glee.

Brutus and Simon removed their helms, and hugged one another again, patting each other on the back. Having finally caught his breath, Brutus grabbed a claymore from the field nearby and presented it to Simon.

"Please, Sir Simon. A worthier opponent I have yet to face. You would honour me greatly by taking this. I can train you to wield two of these, should you have another?"

Simon paused, frowning. "I do. I can't."

Brutus smiled. "I own four of these, big man. You honour me. Please, take it."

Simon grinned widely, from ear to ear, a twinkle in his eyes as he carefully took the presented blade.

"Respect," Simon said simply, locking gauntlets with Brutus once more.

"Respect indeed. You are welcome to train with the Boston Blades any time, good sir. You all are. I'll swap numbers with you, big guy. Be seeing you."

Brutus headed over to the rest of his crew, similarly awestruck by the epic duel of the mountain men they'd just witnessed.

"Well, that was touching," Yvette said from behind the barrier, her sons bouncing up and down nearby.

"Love! You're here. Harold mate, let's head back to camp."

Moments later, the brothers in steel arrived back at camp with Tim's family in tow.

The evening hours were spent in joyous laughter, playing with the kids and more duels and displays. Harry watched smiling as Olivia played hide and seek with the boys. Not too easy, only having two tents to hide in, but they enjoyed it all the same.

"Shh!" Olivia mimicked to Harry as he watched her bent towards him in the entrance to his tent.

"Got you, aunty Olly!" the boys yelled out as they found her.

"Oh, good job, you two. Well now, looks like it's my turn!"

Harry smiled, watching this go on for some time, as Tim came over to join him.

"Right, mate. Yvette is going back with the boys tonight. What are we doing about sleep?"

Harry had all but forgotten. They had two tents, four spaces, and five of them.

"Well, in an ideal world, Olivia would have her own tent. I could try asking the Boston Blades?" Harry suggested.

"No good, mate. Already tried that. Yvette's willing to drop her off. If not, us three will cram into the bigger tent, you'll share with Olly. Can you handle that?"

Harry mulled it over.

"I've come to realise that we're friends, Timothy. I had a video call with Harriet where her latest research convinced me of that."

Tim shrugged. "Long as you're good with it, mate. We'll be fine in the other tent."

"Boys! Stop playing tag, time to go!" Yvette called out, Olivia chasing Steve and Tom round the tents.

"But muuummm!" they cried in unison, Harry chuckling.

174

They rushed over as she clicked her fingers, hugging Harry's leg tightly.

"Bye, uncle Harry! Bye, daddy! We like the flower lady, mummy. Can she come to dinner?" Steve pleaded.

"Yeah, can she? Please, please?" Tom added.

"We'll see, boys. Right, come on then, let's go. Are we taking you home, Olivia?" Yvette asked.

"I'm fine here, thanks, Yvette. Be good for your mother, boys," Olivia added.

"Yes, aunty Olly!" they cheered in unison, Yvette taking them back to the car after firmly kissing Tim on the lips.

"Get a tent, bruv!" Jester mocked, Simon chuckling nearby.

"Speaking of. Bedtime soon, mates, I'm cramming in with you two. Harry will be sleeping with Olly."

"Use protection, bruv," Jester chimed in.

Harry scowled at Jester. "Knock it off!"

Jester and Tim were both howling, as Simon stood sentinel nearby.

"Care," he stated simply.

Harry nodded, taking his gear into the tent, removing it from the racks. They all followed suit as the sun fully set, darkness falling over the castle grounds.

Harry stepped outside, gesturing Olivia in.

"You get changed first, Olivia, I'll just be in my tunic and boxers. All good."

"I don't mind, Harry, you can come in?" she responded.

Harry blushed. "That's OK, call me in when you're ready."

Olivia smiled, headed inside and removed her corset and dress, opting for a large white shift as a nightie.

"Come in, Harry!" she called, met with immature cackling from the nearby tent—followed by an "Ow!

Bruv!" presumably Jester's arm taking a whack from Simon.

Harry joined Olivia inside, as she lay on the cloth beneath, beckoning for him to join her.

He tugged at his collar, chest tightening, joining her nearby.

"Harry?" Olivia whispered as she hugged up next to him, almost exactly as the flash had hit him earlier, strawberry scent lingering in his nose.

"Yeah?"

"Can you finally see me?" she whispered meekly, gazing into his eyes as he stared at the roof of the tent.

"I sure do, Olivia. You're a great employee, but an even greater friend."

Her lips parted as if to say something more, but instead, she simply smiled. She turned to the side, muttering "Goodnight, Harry."

He tugged at his collar once more, turning to his side, ready to sleep. "Sweet dreams, Olivia."

Chapter 29

The morning sun soon woke Harry, the air inside the tent quickly becoming a furnace. He turned to see Olivia already gone, then opened the tent to let the fresh air in.

She'd got to work setting up the display racks once more, her and Harry's gear displayed proudly against the morning sun.

"Morning, Harry!" she beamed, smile not quite reaching her eyes, arms folded across her chest.

"Good morning. You slept even less than I did. Then again, you're always first to the office, so I suppose you're used to it?"

"Exactly, Harry," she responded, returning to her leatherworking kit.

Jester poked his head out of the other tent. "What's all this racket? You two lovebirds woke us up!" he complained.

Harry rolled his eyes. "Go back to sleep, then."

"Can't. Got to go visit the Turdis," Jester said as he hopped out of the tent.

"I wish you wouldn't bloody call it that! It's an insult to both Doctor Who and portaloos!" Harry yelled after Jester as he sprinted off.

"Morning, mates. You behave yourself, Harold?" Tim said, poking his head out of the tent, Olivia ignoring him, content with her leatherwork.

Harry rolled his eyes once more. "Yes, good morning, Timothy. Simon up too?"

"Yeah. He's doing press-ups in there. He doesn't quit, mate!"

Tim almost sounded in awe.

"We didn't plan any fights for today. Any thoughts, lads?" Tim asked.

"Well, I think I'm ready to fight Harry," Olivia said, eyeing up her armour, proudly on display nearby.

"Splendid idea, Olivia. My old broadsword in your hands, versus my new one. I've not even tested the steel yet."

Tim nodded. "Great, that's one bout. We might need a few more. I'll ask Jester once he's back from the Turdis."

"Can you people please stop bloody calling it that!" Harry protested.

"Turdis!" Simon called out from the tent, Harry sighing as Tim howled with laughter.

A crowd began to form, vendors all set up from the day before, the medieval merriment continuing.

"Harry, bruv, armour up. You too, Olly. Let's get a crowd going," Jester said, handing Harry his helm.

He fastened it tight as Jester helped Olivia affix her plate mail. A small crowd began to gather nearby, weapons drawn, Olivia and Harry taking the field.

Harry tightened his grip on the broadsword, new steel still untested in his hands. Olivia stood opposite, helm gleaming in the sun, his old Viking blade raised high.

"Lay on arms!" Jester called, voice ringing across the field.

The first clash rang out sharp, Olivia meeting him with surprising force. Her movements were fluid, but edged with something more—each blow just a little harder than necessary, each step pressing Harry back faster than he expected.

Harry chuckled through the strain. "Not so rough, Olivia!"

Olivia said nothing, only drove him further, her blade hammering down until his shoulders ached.

He caught her sword in a guard and twisted, forcing her aside. "Yield!" he called, breathless.

But Olivia didn't stop. She ripped free, hammering again, forcing Harry back step after step, steel clanging furiously. Her chest heaved, a low sound breaking from her throat as she swung for his helm.

"Fight over!" Simon's bellow cracked across the field, louder than the blades themselves.

Olivia froze. Her sword hung inches from Harry's spaulder. For a heartbeat, she just stared at him, eyes shadowed behind the visor. Then, with a gasp, she lowered the weapon and stumbled back.

"Sorry, Harry! I—I got carried away."

Harry's chest felt tight as he gasped and chuckled. "No harm done. Fierce, Olivia. Spirited but undisciplined."

Olivia dipped into an elegant curtsy, lips smiling but her eyes downcast. "Of course, Harry."

The crowd clapped politely. Only Simon lingered, gaze hard, watching Olivia far more closely than Harry did, massive arms folded across his chest.

"Right, good fight, but we can do better. Si, bruv, can I borrow this?" Jester asked as he grabbed the hilt of Simon's zweihander.

His arms quickly buckled under the weight of it, sliding it back into the rack.

"Maybe not. Christ, Si, just how strong are you?"

"Lorry mechanic!" Simon laughed deep, grabbing both his claymores.

"I've got it!" Jester declared. "A grand melee. The five of us. You three, broadswords. Me and Si dual wielding. It'll be epic, innit!"

"Brothers in steel!" the four of them announced, affixing their helms as Olivia sighed.

Word of the unusual melee spread quickly across the castle grounds. Other reenactors abandoned their displays, drawn by whispers of "five fighters" and "dual wielding madness." The crowd that had gathered for the previous bout doubled, then tripled.

"Bloody hell, look at this mob," Tim muttered through his visor as they took their positions.

From across the field, Brutus himself approached with several Boston Blades members. "Five-way melee with dual wielding? Bring the popcorn, boys," he called out.

Phones appeared held high throughout the crowd as word continued to spread, with several food vendors shutting shop to attend.

Simon stood in the centre, a claymore in each massive hand, grinning beneath his helm. The others formed a loose circle around him—Harry with his new broadsword, Tim with his own broadsword, Olivia with the Viking blade, and Jester spinning his twin daggers.

"Last one standing wins!" Jester announced to the crowd. "No quarter asked, none given!"

The spectators pressed closer to the barriers, anticipation crackling through the air.

"I'll step in to marshal," Brutus boomed, crossing the barrier. "Lay on arms!"

Chaos erupted immediately.

Simon became the prime target—four fighters converging on the dual-wielding giant. His claymores swept in wide arcs, keeping them at bay whilst steel rang against steel in a symphony of clashing metal that echoed across the field.

Harry struck high whilst Tim went low, but Simon caught Harry's blade on his left sword while bringing his right down to parry Tim's thrust. The impact sent vibrations through the hilts, but Simon held firm, strong as steel.

Jester darted in from behind, daggers flashing, but Simon sensed the movement and spun, his claymore whistling past Jester's helm by inches. The crowd gasped.

"He's got eyes in the back of his head!" someone shouted, the crowd growing even further.

Olivia pressed her attack, her Viking blade hammering down on Simon's guard. For a moment, the two were locked, steel grinding against steel, before Simon twisted and sent her stumbling backward.

The brothers tried to coordinate, Harry feinting left whilst Tim struck right, but Simon's reach advantage kept them both at distance. His claymores moved like extensions of his arms—one defending whilst the other attacked in fluid, deadly arcs.

Jester changed tactics, using his speed to stay mobile, striking and retreating before the heavier weapons could catch him. His daggers found gaps in the melee, forcing the others to watch multiple threats as he lunged towards the brothers.

"Look at that footwork!" Brutus called out appreciatively. "You'll be training me, big man!"

The crowd was entranced as the five fighters danced around one another in a glorious storm of steel. Simon's power dominated the centre whilst the others circled like vultures, looking for openings and pecking one another.

Harry and Olivia found themselves fighting side by side, their blades working in tandem to pressure Simon's left flank. For a moment, it seemed they had him—but Simon pivoted, bringing both claymores down in a devastating cross-pattern that caught both their weapons simultaneously.

The shock of the impact sent Olivia's sword flying from her hands. It clattered across the ground as she stumbled and fell to one knee.

"Olly's out!" Jester announced. The crowd applauded as she curtsied and retreated to the side.

Four remained.

Tim seized the moment of Simon's extended guard to rush in close, but Simon anticipated it. He dropped his right claymore entirely and caught Tim in a bear hug, lifting him clean off the ground before gently setting him down outside the combat area.

"Tim yields!" The crowd roared with laughter and approval.

Three left in the fight, Simon still standing strong.

They circled one another, starting to tire, breathing heavily beneath their helms. Jester darted in low with both daggers, outplayed by Harry who struck him in the side as his guard was open.

"Damn it, Harry! I'm out!" Jester announced, ditching his daggers and retreating to the sides with the others.

Only Harry and Simon remained.

Simon grinned deep, teeth baring behind his helm. "Regret!" he roared at Harry, now alone against the behemoth, Simon retrieving his second blade.

Harry's heart pounded in his chest, now facing off alone against Simon. He was bigger, stronger, fitter, just plain better—but Harry was no coward, and wouldn't yield unearned.

Simon went fully on the offensive, sweeping at Harry with both blades, a furious storm of steel.

The aggressive assault drove Harry back, but it left Simon slightly off-balance. Harry saw his chance and lunged forward, his broadsword narrowly missing Simon's pauldron.

The crowd roared as the duel continued. Simon was stronger, more experienced, but Harry noticed something—the big man's breathing was getting heavier. The sustained defence against multiple opponents was beginning to take its toll.

Harry changed his strategy. Instead of trying to overpower Simon, he began to move more, making the giant work harder to track him. Circle left, feint right, force Simon to keep turning those massive claymores.

Simon's swings began to slow slightly. Not much, but Harry's trained eye caught it. Years of psychological observation had taught him to notice small changes in behaviour and energy, and his focus felt extra sharp today. He wanted the win. He needed the win. He would fight to the bitter end.

The crowd sensed the shift. What began as David versus Goliath was becoming a test of endurance versus patience.

Simon made a powerful overhead strike with both claymores. Harry stepped aside, instead of blocking, letting the claymores strike the ground. For just a flash, Simon was overextended.

Harry took his chance, tapping his broadsword against Simon's breastplate.

"Fight over!" Brutus roared.

The crowd exploded as Simon dropped his weapons and embraced Harry, lifting him despite his exhaustion.

"Brothers in steel!" Simon rumbled.

"Brothers in arms! Brothers in steel!" the brothers and Jester parroted back, all gathering around and hugging with metallic clangs as the crowd slowly began to disperse.

Olivia had once again positioned herself to answer questions from onlookers as the brothers sat themselves down to rest.

"Nothing that happens today will top that, Si," Jester declared, helm removed and racked.

They all removed their armour, muscles aching and displays done for the day. They tore down their tents with methodical precision, packing their gear away. Brutus and the Boston Blades left to do similar.

"We should invite him to swords sometime," Harry stated. "Now I've finally toppled our own Goliath, I want a crack at the behemoth!"

Simon laughed deep, chest rumbling. "Rematch."

Harry gulped as the others chuckled hard.

The rest of the afternoon was spent visiting some of the other displays and food stalls, shortly before they closed themselves. The medieval event had been a roaring success, but once again finished for another year.

"I'm almost loath to go back to work tomorrow after the weekend we've just had," Harry said as they gathered around their vehicles, ready to depart. "Anyone need a lift back?"

Olivia smiled, raising her hand meekly, approaching the passenger side of Harry's car.

"Nah, bruv, I'm going with the big man. What did I tell you boys? You two got to get on me and Si's level. You've shown me today you can do that, Harry. I'm proud, bruv, really."

Harry smiled warmly back to Jester. "I'm proud of you too, Jester. That means a lot. I'll call you tomorrow. Everyone, let me know you get home safe in the group chat, please. Brothers in steel!"

"Brothers in steel!" they roared back, everyone heading off for home.

Harry gripped the wheel with one hand, leaned back in his chair, relaxed by the sound of the tyres humming against the road.

Olivia's phone buzzed in her lap. She glanced at it, quickly dismissing it, turning it upside down.

"Did you have a good time then, Olivia?" Harry asked.

"I did, thank you. Enlightening."

Not the word he'd have chosen, but glad she found it educational nonetheless. They spent the rest of the drive in comfortable silence, pulling up outside Olivia's flat, roof tile finally fallen to the floor and broken.

"Want a hand with your kit bag, Olivia?" Harry asked.

"That would be lovely. Thank you, Harry," she said, as they hopped out of the car.

The weight of the bag pressed against Harry's already aching shoulder, grunting as he brought it through her door. He was greeted by the colours, the photos, the familiar scent of strawberries.

"See you tomorrow, Harry," she said, smiling as she gestured to the door.

"Sweet dreams, Olivia."

Back home, more than ready for bed.

Chapter 30

The dreadful wailing of Barbie Girl felt particularly menacing this Monday morning. Harry groaned, dragging himself out of bed to silence the alarm, his muscles still aching from Sunday's melee. The victory over Simon felt like a distant memory now, replaced by the familiar dread of returning routine.

He dragged himself through his morning ritual—cold shower, shave, suit—each feeling heavier than the last. The weekend had been exciting, but now came the inevitable crash back to earth, an entire year before their next castle event.

Harry pushed open the office door, Olivia typing away at her desk. "Morning, Olivia," he said, glancing toward her as she focused intently on her computer screen.

"Morning, Harry" she replied briefly, quickly looking back at her screen.

Harry paused at her desk. Something felt different. Off. "How are you feeling after the weekend? Still coming down from the excitement?"

"Fine, thanks. Yeah, definitely." her fingers still tapping at the keyboard.

Harry frowned slightly and headed into his office. The familiar mahogany desk, the bookshelf, the client chairs—everything looked the same, but something essential was missing. The usual spread of pastries that had become as much a part of his morning routine as coffee.

He poked his head back out. "Olivia, did we forget the cinnamon swirls today?"

"Oh." She looked up, blinking as if surprised. "Sorry, I forgot to pick them up. Bit tired after the weekend, it was soul-crushing."

"Right, of course. Post-event blues." Harry tried to smile. "I'll just grab something at lunch."

"OK Harry." She was already looking back at her screen.

Harry returned to his office feeling oddly unsettled. He'd grown more accustomed to Olivia's daily attentions than he'd realised. Without the warm pastries, the enthusiastic greetings, the constant anticipation of his needs, the office felt a little cold.

Harry went through the motions with his first client, offered the standard advice, but his heart wasn't in it. The man left looking as deflated as Harry felt.

Around noon, Harry's stomach began to rumble. Usually, Olivia would have appeared by now with some lunch, but his office door remained closed. He checked his phone—no messages about lunch plans, no cheerful updates about her day either.

Harry walked to her desk. "Fancy grabbing some lunch? Fish and chips?"

"I brought something from home," she said, not looking away from her computer. "You go ahead."

"Right."

Harry grabbed himself fish and chips from the stall on the promenade, but found himself full after only a few bites. His appetite seemed consumed by the post event blues. Not even the salty sea air was relaxing today.

The afternoon dragged. Another whiskey barrel case, then a cryptocurrency scam that blurred together with all the others. Without Olivia's usual interruptions—bringing tea, asking about his cases, sharing little observations about their clients—the day felt endless and monotonous.

At five o'clock sharp, Olivia appeared at his door. "I'm heading off now, Harry. See you tomorrow."

"Have a lovely evening." Harry looked up from his paperwork. "Everything alright? You seem a bit distant today."

"Just tired, Harry. The weekend was quite intense, wasn't it?"

"True, but it was exciting, at least. Well, rest up. Tomorrow's another day."

"True. Goodnight, Harry."

After she left, Harry sat in his office feeling strangely hollow. The ticking metronome of the analogue clock felt oppressive in a way it never had before. He realised how much of his daily routine had become intertwined with Olivia's presence—her enthusiasm, her care, her constant attention to his comfort. Was this what Harriet had warned him about?

Uncannily timed, his phone buzzed with a text from Harriet:

> *"Hope you had a lovely Monday, darling. Looking forward to our cinema date Friday. Harriet x"*

For the first time all day, Harry felt a genuine smile spread across his face. At least someone was excited to see him, someone who appreciated his craft and looked forward to their time together.

He tapped back:

> *"Monday was rather flat, to be honest. These post-event blues are hitting harder than expected. Or perhaps I'm reaping the benefits of not appreciating my friends enough. Harry"*

Her reply came quickly:

> *"Poor darling. The comedown after such highs is*
> *always difficult. Just think—Friday we'll have our*
> *own private celebration. I can't wait to finally*
> *meet you properly. Harriet x"*

Harry read the message twice, feeling warmth spread through his chest. Yes, Friday would be different. Friday would be special.

He packed up his things and headed home, telling himself that tomorrow Olivia would be back to her usual self, that this was just a temporary adjustment period.

But he couldn't shake the feeling that something fundamental had shifted, and he wasn't sure how to get it back.

At home, even Mr. Snuffles seemed less comforting than usual. Harry held the stuffed rabbit close, staring at the ceiling, wondering why the taste of victory had turned so quickly to ash in his mouth.

The week stretched ahead of him, leading to Friday's promised reunion with intellectual companionship and genuine connection. He just had to get through the next few days of this strange, cold distance that had settled over his daily routine like fog over the Norfolk sea.

Chapter 31

The week dragged on, every day much the same as Monday. It passed by in a blur of whiskey, false romance and forgotten pastries.

Olivia remained tepid towards Harry the entire week, scuffing his theory of post-event blues. He tried to consider if he'd slighted her himself, or if she was going through something significant. He sighed, sat at his bedroom desk thinking about it.

He was just glad for work to be over for the week. It had deflated him, quite possibly to the point of not wanting his date tonight.

He pulled out his phone, sighing deeply.

"Harriet, I'm sorry. I can't do this."

Moments later, his phone buzzed with a reply.

"Unacceptable, darling. I've prepared extensively for tonight. Now what's all this about then?"

He flipped the phone in his hands, fumbling for words that wouldn't come. He shrugged, deciding simply to call her instead. It rang several times, but clicked to voicemail, as another text came through.

"Hold on—let's have a video chat."

Harry fired up his laptop, spotting Dr Baker online. He hit the video call button, which she cancelled—then quickly called him back. Harry chuckled, wondering if she might have been a hidden control freak.

"Harry, darling, there you are. So sorry, I hit the wrong button. For all my academics I'm still only human after all! So come on then, what's going on? Why are you cancelling on me?"

Harry laughed, grateful for the honest humanity.

"I'm sorry, Harriet, I didn't mean to disappoint. I've had a tough week. I think I've alienated a friend—either that, or she has something going on and won't share it with me."

Harriet stared at him from behind the thick rims of her glasses, dressed almost precisely the same as their first call, professional ponytail and all.

"I see. Who is this friend, exactly?"

"My secretary, actually. She's become a close friend. I value her, just like the research we discussed last time. I tried to show her that, and I think I just upset her."

"Have you considered, darling, that she may see you as more than just a friend? The way she takes care of you doesn't sound like professional devotion or simple friendship to me."

Harry clutched at his T-shirt, looking for a tie to loosen.

"We had that talk. She knows there are professional boundaries I cannot cross, as her employer. I have a moral obligation, too—I'm twice her age, Harriet. In what world would that be OK?"

"In her world, Harry."

Harry sighed. "But not in mine."

There was a moment of silence between them as Harriet looked off camera, appearing to retrieve something. He couldn't make it out with the background blurred.

"Well, in that case, Harry, I think you leave me no choice. I'll just have to make you mine," Harriet began, now openly flirting with him.

Harry's melancholy was quickly shoved aside by a little hope, but hope hadn't quite won out yet.

"I'm... well, look, I'm not up for the movies, but we could have a little film date and dinner at mine?" Harry suggested, voice cracking a little.

"Absolutely. I'll be right there."

Harriet closed the call, leaving Harry grinning at his laptop as he drifted off into his imagination. He imagined them sat together on his sofa, watching his favourite film, sharing popcorn as Morpheus explained objective reality to Neo.

Minutes passed as another video call came in—once more from Harriet.

"Harry, darling. I'm so sorry. My stupid car won't start!"

Harry sighed, red pill swallowed, reality setting back in.

"No! Well, look, what if I buy you a taxi or something?"

"No, no. That's a lot of money and a long way, and to be honest, I only drive myself—I've never so much as sat in a taxi, and lovely as you are, I'm not starting now."

Harry rolled his eyes. Perhaps a little bit of a control freak after all. But he could work with that.

"I could come to you?" he suggested.

"Again, Harry—a little soon. I'm starting to second-guess this," she responded, a little curt.

Harry sighed. "All right. Maybe next time, then?"

Harriet grinned. "You're not off the hook that easily, mister. I said I would make you mine and I meant it. Grab some alcohol. You're going to sit right here with me, watch a movie, and get blind drunk. Acceptable?"

Harry grinned, already rushing off to grab the beer and the vodka.

"Have you seen The Matrix?" he asked.

"No, but I'd seen it was streaming. How retro! I'm happy to watch it with you, darling. I'll get the wine poured right away. You can take a shot to get you going."

Harry happily obliged, knocking back a shot of vodka—bitter and burning.

"Ready, darling?" Harriet asked, glass of wine on her desk.

Harry settled into his chair, burning sensation of vodka still lingering on his tongue. He cracked open a beer, satisfying *hiss* as he felt the cold metal under his thumb. A green cascade of code falling down the screen, The Matrix beginning.

"Harry, darling, take a shot when Neo takes the pill!" Harriet suggested with a giggle.

Harry chuckled, obliging. Vodka burnt a little less this time, hiss filling his ears from his second beer. Or third, possibly, he wasn't sure.

"Falling behind, darling. Another shot for you," Harriet suggested, her glass still full—or recently refilled. Harry wasn't paying attention—more engrossed in her wicked smile, and wicked pair of...personalities. Wicked personality. That ponytail, too.

Harry relaxed further into his chair, another shot downed, another hiss. Room felt warm, comfy, watching Neo skillfully dodge bullets. Except those two, sadly.

"More shots, darling!" Harriet announced, Harry's hand moving before his brain agreed. He'd started knocking them back as and when at this point. *Hiss.*

"Harry my love, you doing alright?" Harriet sounded warm, concerned.

"Never...Never better!" Harry slurred. Oh dear, when had that started? *Hiss.*

"Well, as psychologists both, I'm sure we have our own interpretations of many events in that film. I have to be honest, Harry—I would choose the red pill, seeing the truth in all its flawed but beautiful nakedness. You strike me as a blue pill kind of guy. Correct?"

Harry thought for a moment, train wobbling on the tracks, room gently swaying.

"Oh yeah. I'm all about that blue pill life," Harry said, words catching against his thick tongue, staring at his beautiful date through the screen. *Hiss.*

Harriet grinned deeply, refilling her wine glass. No, it was already full. Wasn't it?

"Well, you know, Harry, I thought Neo and Trinity had some real chemistry. Some real, I don't know—sexual energy. I wanted them to rip each other's clothes off and go at it like a pair of rabbits far, far sooner. Didn't you?"

Was this flirting? Was he, was this happening? Harry grinned wide, imagining such a scenario between himself and Harriet—Mr Snuffles, his own rabbit, carelessly chucked aside. He was a little sad she wasn't there with him.

Hiss.

"Ah—" Harry began, briefly stopping himself before continuing. "Ifh you were here, that could be ush!" Harry blurted, knocking back another vodka shot—nope, carpet drank that one. Oops.

Luckily for him, it landed.

"Well now, Harry. Forward, but confident. I like it. You know, it would be a bit of a shame for me to put all this glamouring up I did to waste now, wouldn't it?"

Harriet began to slowly unbutton her blouse, sobering Harry up significantly as he watched enthralled, pulse beating a samba in his ears. Fine personalities indeed.

"Well? What do you think, Harry?"

Harry's mouth was dry as a bone, beer cans staring from the wobbly desk. Harry couldn't think about much right now. It had been years since he'd seen a woman even this level of naked, and as far as he hoped, she was just getting started.

"Oh! I approve! I very much approve! Those are beautiful. You are, I mean," Harry fumbled around with his words, met with a wide grin from Harriet.

"Right then, handsome. I think it's your turn. Come on, let's see what I'm in for, shall we?"

Without thinking, inebriated Harry stood up and dropped his trousers. He quickly became embarrassed and pulled them back up again.

"Oh, very nice, Harry. Very respectable. Well, to be continued on our next date in person, I think. Sweet dreams, Harry!"

Harry closed his laptop, thud too loud in his ears. Tried to stand, legs were jelly. Hand on desk, then wall, then doorframe, then finally stumbled over to his bed. Collapsed atop it, his face aching from smiling. Room spun in circles, Mr Snuffles an anchor in the stormy sea. Eyes closed, green matrix code wobbling beneath them, then—nothing.

Chapter 32

Harry woke up feeling groggy, tired and hungover. The chirping birds outside might as well have been woodpeckers skilfully drilling holes in his skull.

Harry sat on the side of his bed, grinning happily at Mr Snuffles. His phone had a text waiting:

> *"I had a wonderful night last night, big boy. I look forward to seeing you again real soon. Harriet x"*

Harry flipped the phone in his hand, considering his reply, grin stretching from ear to ear.

> *"There's a long and lonely weekend ahead of us. Perhaps we should meet?"*

After some moments, a reply buzzed through.

> *"Tempting, but a busy weekend for me, darling, plus my car needs some love. Let's make a movie date for next Friday, I'm sure it'll be sorted by then. Harriet x"*

Harry sighed. They clearly liked each other, and clearly a lot. What began as intellectually stimulating conversation had clearly formed an attraction, a developing bond—one that he was more than ready for.

As the woodpeckers hammered at his skull, he formed an idea. He remembered reading about a book signing in Norwich today, and it being a Saturday he was free to attend. Dr Harriet Baker would be in attendance, and Harry could sweep her off her feet.

It was a bold move, for sure, but a romantic one—and Neo wanted his Trinity. The butterflies in his stomach fluttered at the possibilities.

Wasting no time, he rushed to get ready, trying on a dozen outfits before settling for a simple open-collar shirt and jeans. Not too formal, not too casual—perfect.

He pulled into the car park, buzzing with energy even after the irritating task of grabbing a ticket—followed by the similarly arduous task of finding a free parking spot.

Every step towards the bookshop moved a mountain. He began to second-guess himself—was this a fool's errand? Was this love? He almost turned back, stopping himself a few times as he drew closer and closer to the bookshop.

This was it. He had to know, and he had to know now. He breathed deep, closing his eyes as he pressed his hand against the glass pane of the door.

There she sat, beautiful and neat, large-rimmed glasses and tightly tied ponytail. There was no queue— he raced right over, her beaming a smile.

"Harriet! It's me! I came!" he croaked, voice husky with dread.

"Aww. Well hello, me. Sign your book?"

"Oh, um, yes please. So I know you were... hesitant about us meeting so soon, and I'm sorry I came here— but I just had to see you."

Harriet narrowed her gaze, smile fading. "I'm sorry? Have we met? Anyway, 'me', what name is it for your book?"

"I... It's... Harry."

One hastily scrawled signature later, she handed the book back to Harry.

"There you are. Are you OK? You look like you've seen a ghost."

The walls began to close in around him, the footsteps outside echoing through his mind, his soul. He began to breathe, harder, faster, heavier—the room spinning, faster and faster until he flopped into a heap on the floor.

"Gosh! Hold on!"

Harriet rushed over, helping Harry up. "You there, go get the gentleman a glass of water, won't you?"

The nearby shopkeeper obliged, heading into the back, as Harriet took Harry to sit down.

"Breathe. Stay calm. Harry, wasn't it? Just breathe in, breathe out. That's it, keep that up. Here."

Harry practically downed the water he was given, slowly and methodically breathing in, and out, time and time again, for what felt like a small eternity.

"What's happening, Harry? You seem to know me. But I don't know you at all—I'm sorry."

Harry handed her a business card, still not able to speak, as he fumbled around for his phone, hands trembling.

"Harry Maxwell. You're familiar, I've interacted with a client or two of yours in my research, and I've read a book of yours. But no, sorry, can't say we've met."

Harry handed her the phone carefully, his hands trembling and shaking, his body begging to shut down, his mind screaming.

"What's this? Oh... oh my. You've been texting with someone pretending to be me, it seems. Oh, I'm so sorry, darling. This must be heartbreaking for you. I need you to report this profile, when you're able to come to your senses—that is most definitely not myself. I'm so, so sorry."

Harry began to openly cry, the shopkeeper corralling them into a staff area in the back.

"Wait here, OK? I've books to sign, then I'll be back."

Harry sat shaking, convulsing on his chair in the staff room, the light from the overhead fluorescent light piercing into his soul. He could barely think, barely concentrate. He breathed in deep, counted to ten, breathed out again.

He did this for some time, the shaking finally stopped, the tears ran dry. Harriet, the real Harriet, came back into the staff room and sat beside him, arm around his shoulder.

"Right, well. I'm afraid I've got to go soon, as I have to present a paper at a conference. Are you going to be OK?"

Harry swallowed deep, nodding. He tried to speak, words escaping him.

"That's OK, dear. Take your time, head home, get some rest. I'll be off then. Best of luck, Harry."

Just like that, she was gone. The woman he'd been texting with, been sharing deep, intellectually stimulating conversation with, moments and movies with was gone.

Except she wasn't gone. That was a total stranger. He'd been scammed, well and truly, just the same as any one of his clients.

But the hammer hadn't dropped yet. The knife was stuck in, but it wasn't twisted. Whoever they were, whatever they wanted—he was yet to know.

He stumbled back to his car, one foot after another. He sat in the driver's seat, sobbing and shaking once more.

He'd told himself he was the expert. That he could see the angles, the traps, the lies. Harry Maxwell, scam counsellor—a client of his own making.

Chapter 33

Harry hadn't slept a wink that night. An hour or two, here and there perhaps, but he was jolted awake repeatedly with the memory of Dr Baker at the book signing asking if they'd met. The confusion on her face dug into his ribs like a dagger.

He lay there, staring at the ceiling, Mr Snuffles clutched against his chest like a shield, protecting him from reality. Every conversation with "Harriet" now replayed in his mind with sickening clarity.

The intellectual discussions that had seemed so profound. The personal revelations he'd shared. Friday night's video call. It looked and sounded precisely like her. Either she had a twin sister she didn't know about, or he was dealing with some seriously advanced technology—and scammers.

But that was exactly it—the knife still hung there, untwisted. No scam—and there had been plenty of opportunity. The car breaking down story, for instance— he'd foolishly offered to pay for a taxi, probably would have offered to pay for the car repairs if needed. But they didn't want money. So what the hell did they want?

His phone buzzed on the bedside table. Harry's heart raced as he saw the notification.

"Good morning, darling! Hope you're having a lovely Sunday. I've been thinking about Friday night... when shall we do it again? Harriet x"

The casual tone, the pet names, the implied intimacy—it all felt like acid now, bile rising in his stomach. Harry stared at the message, his hands shaking. Who was this person? What did they want? Why had they chosen him?

He stared at his list of contacts, looking at Tim, finger hovering above the call button. He wanted his brother, but what would he even say?

He pocketed the phone and stumbled to his desk, opening his laptop with trembling hands. He thought back to the red and blue pill conversation with fake Harriet. How he wished he could swallow that blue pill right now and go back to the comfort of his fabricated reality.

Harry opened his laptop and pulled up the dating app. 'Dr Harriet Baker' with her warm smile and academic credentials. The profile that had seemed so genuine, so perfect. He scrolled through their message history, now seeing manipulation where he'd once seen connection.

Whoever he was dealing with—they were smart. Every bit as intelligent as he, if not more so. Clearly an academic, too—they understood psychology in a way that rivalled or even exceeded his own expertise.

That expertise kicked in despite his melancholy. Was this random? Or was this targeted? It felt as if someone had studied him, learnt his vulnerabilities, crafted the perfect persona to exploit him.

Three questions persisted. Who, how, and why?

He started with how. Tired, exhausted, downright miserable but he was a scientist, an academic, a researcher.

He tugged at his collar as he tapped away at his keyboard, searching, scouring the corners of the internet for tales of technologies, fake personas, cloned voices and faces.

One deep dive into deepfake technology later, he understood the how, at least to an extent. How many clients had sat in his office as he regurgitated the same, predictable, pragmatic advice when his grasp on technology, on modern scam techniques had clearly slipped?

It made sense, too. Dr Harriet Baker was a public enough figure. Not famous or overly well known, but there were plenty of pictures and videos of her online from recorded lectures and conferences, so plenty of reference material to create a convincing facsimile.

His scammer could be one of her students, perhaps, though their grasp of psychology suggested graduate-level understanding—possibly even masters level themselves.

Harry yawned deep, drumming his fingers on his desk, glaring at the screen as it glared right back, burning his tired eyes.

His phone buzzed again.

"You're quiet, darling. Everything all right? I know Friday was disappointing with my car troubles, but we had such a lovely evening instead. Harriet x"

The concern seemed genuine, but Harry now knew it was performative. Every word calculated. Every emotion manufactured. The word "darling" cut him like a blade's edge.

He tried to think logically. Who would want to catfish him? Who had the technical skills and psychological knowledge to pull this off so effectively?

Harry spent the day spiralling through possibilities, each more paranoid than the last. Every stranger he'd encountered recently became suspect. Every casual conversation now seemed loaded with hidden meaning. His family, his friends, the guy who sells him fish and chips on the promenade, his smile just a little too wide.

He couldn't eat. Couldn't focus. Could barely manage a proper thought. Even thinking of fish and chips made him want to vomit.

Even Tim's voice hovered in his head. Warm, familiar, but edged with suspicion. What if he knew? Jester, needing the money? Stoic Simon? Even kind Olivia?

Every face blurred into the same. Harriet's smile, her glasses, her voice—she was everywhere.

The worst part wasn't the deception itself—it was the intimacy of it. They'd fattened the pig, now ripe for the butchering.

His phone buzzed throughout the day with messages from 'Harriet'—cheerful updates about her Sunday, attempts to make impossible plans, casual references to their 'relationship.' Each message another dagger in the ribs.

His phone buzzed once more.

"Sweet dreams, Harry. I can't wait to see what tomorrow brings. Harriet x"

Harry stared at the message, rage building in his chest. Tomorrow would indeed bring something, but not what this fraudster expected. Tomorrow, he would seek answers.

He didn't know who was behind the deception, but he knew one thing with certainty: they had made a mistake targeting him. He pressed his palms flat on the desk, the wood solid beneath his shaking hands. Enough.

Tomorrow, behind his mahogany desk, he would drag this "Harriet" into the light—and unmask the stranger who had shattered his hopes and dreams.

Chapter 34

Sleep proved largely elusive once more, an hour or two here or there.

Even the gulls cawing outside were in on it. Did they know? Were they watching him too? It almost sounded like they were laughing at him.

Harry chewed at his fingernails, Mr Snuffles hugged close as he trembled and shook.

He had to get it together. He breathed in deep, counted to ten, exhaled. Again, and again.

He went through the motions—shower, shave, suit. Picked out his favourite blue silk tie. Somehow, it felt important.

He arrived at the office more than two hours early, startled to see Olivia already there at her desk, tapping away.

She practically jumped out of her chair. "Harry! You surprised me, sorry. You're early? Really early. Are you OK?"

Harry looked her over, wordless, his lips trembling, eyes leaking. He began to cry.

Olivia ditched her desk, rushed over and hugged him tight.

"Shh... Harry... What happened? Are you OK?"

He allowed himself to hug her back, briefly for a moment, strawberry scents battling against the rising bile.

"I will be. Sorry, Olivia. Can you cancel my appointments today, please? Then you can go home."

Olivia frowned, looking up at him, twinkle in her eyes. "What happened, Harry? Is it your auntie?"

Harry didn't answer, he simply walked past into his office, the smell of sugary sweet cinnamon once more hitting his nose, like the return of an old friend. At least Olivia was feeling more like herself again.

Still, the temptation was gone, and hunger was a distant memory. He sat at his desk, fired up the computer, and felt his hands pressed flat against the smooth mahogany desk, closing his eyes.

Breathe in, count to ten, breathe out.

He fumbled in his pocket, hands trembling as he grabbed his phone.

> *"Good morning, darling. Have a great day. Call later? Harriet x"*

Bile once more rising in his throat, 'darling' once more buzzing around his brain like a furious wasp, stinging, stabbing as he shook the word from his mind.

> *"I know you're a fraud."*

His thumb hovered above the send button for some time, as his heart raced, breath quickening. Should he do this? What did he have to gain?

What did he have to lose. Sent.

Moments passed, message delivered. There was no telling when fake Harriet would even see it.

Heard the front door close. Olivia gone home, presumably. Somehow he felt stronger for it, like he had to face this alone. The suit, the tie, the mahogany desk—he wore them like armour.

Harry stared at his own message as time ticked away, the analogue clock a tolling bell in his ears.

Finally, at long last, his phone buzzed.

"Excuse me, darling? Harriet x"

Harry's heart skipped a beat, breathing shallow. Showtime.

"You're no more Harriet than I am the fucking tooth fairy. Cut the crap. Who are you, and what do you want from me?"

He didn't even pause, didn't hesitate as he mashed his thumb on send, adrenaline surging through his veins. Take that, you evil cow.

"Harry, you're not well. Do you need some help, darling? Harriet x"

Harry slammed his fist against the desk, face contorting into a furious scowl.

"I went to the real Dr Baker's book signing. Cut the crap. Who the fuck are you?"

Harry almost wished he had a punch bag in his office, so he could blow off some of the steam pouring from his ears.

More time passed, Harry breathing in deep, counting to ten, breathing out.

"Fine. You've got me. But I've got you, too."

Chills surged through Harry, eyes opened wide, screen burning his eyes. What the hell did that mean?

"Explain yourself. Who are you? What do you want from me?"

His phone buzzed almost instantly.

"Everything."

He dropped his phone on the desk, suddenly a brick of molten lava, convulsing and shaking. The word repeated, a bell tolling through his very soul. *Everything. Everything.*

The word burrowed in deep. Breathe in. Ten. Out.

He grabbed his phone once more, calming his trembling hands.

> *"Too bad. I know you're a fraud, and you hold nothing over me now. I would've paid for your imaginary car troubles too, if you'd asked. Honestly, I'm impressed—you are good. Brilliant, even. But not good enough."*

He mashed send, breathing a big, deep sigh of relief, grin plastered on his face.

> *"Check your email."*

The grin evaporated as quickly as it had appeared, terror taking its place.

One new email from fake Harriet, subject line *"Think of your family".*

A video attachment. His whole body convulsed, shook, trembled as he clicked play.

Oh. Oh *no.*

Oh dear God, *no.*

There they were, Friday film night, together on the video call. He'd barely remembered, with all that had happened.

They got drunk together. They shared a... moment. A moment where she unbuttoned her shirt and he... He...

There he was, in all his glory, trousers down and exposed for the world to see. Tears leaked quickly and furiously from his face, spilling carelessly onto the mahogany below as the bell continued to toll, second after second, from the metronomic analogue clock on the wall.

He could bear it no longer. The frozen frame of his shame hung on the screen, burning his eyes like hot coals.

Shit.

Chapter 35

Everything.

Harry's blood turned to ice in his veins. The word repeated in time with the tolling of the bell from the analogue clock on the wall.

He closed the video with the frozen frame of his shame, trembling hands flat on the mahogany desk.

Think of your family, her email subject had read. If it even was a her?

> *"I've worked with enough clients in my position to know what happens next. You ask for money, I send it, but you release that video anyway. That about right?"*

He hovered over send for a beat, hand shaking, then hit it.

Moments passed, seconds stretched. His throat dry and hoarse, as if he'd been screaming, but not a word had left his lips since morning.

> *"You know what, Harry? Time to take the red pill, darling. Down the rabbit hole you go. How else can I make you see? You were always so stubborn, so blind. Well, it's time Harry. Say goodnight. You're about to be famous! Smile for the cameras!"*

Harry called her number immediately after the text arrived. Straight to voicemail.

He tried again. And again. Each attempt met with the same generic recorded message.

He tapped on his phone desperately:

"Please. Please, I'm begging you! Just stop this! Please!"

But no replies came. Harriet had gone silent, and Harry knew his fate was sealed.

He spent the next hour pacing his office like a caged animal, phone in hand, checking it once per minute. The executioner was taking his time.

An hour of silence. Harry's phone sat on the mahogany desk, screen dark, bomb waiting to explode.

The fuse lit. Screen came to life.

One new notification.

Susan Mayweather, next appointment cancelled. Smell of whiskey burnt in his memory, staring at the cancellation. Maybe it was unrelated. Maybe—

Phone buzzed again. James Moore, appointment cancelled. Teacher with the teenage daughter. God, his daughter. Had she—

Phone buzzed again. And again, and again and again. Bomb detonated, but hadn't the good grace to kill him with it, watching it buzz his world to dust in real time. Text messages came flying in:

Tim: "Harold, what the fuck is this mate?"

Yvette: "Harry, how could you? The children—"

Simon: "Disappointing."

Jester: "Bruv, what have you done? This ain't funny Harry."

214

His email pinged relentlessly. LinkedIn flooded with stranger requests. Google reviews: *"Pervert."* *"Disgusting." "Would not recommend."*

More client cancellations poured in:

"I'm cancelling my appointment."

"Sickening."

"I can't be associated with this."

"How can you counsel anyone when you clearly need help yourself?"

The video was everywhere. Posted to his business Facebook page, shared in local community groups, sent directly to his contact list. His hands shook as he stared at his screen. Maybe it wasn't so bad. Maybe it could be contained, and there was no iceberg. Maybe he could come back from this.

Typed his own name into the search engine. "Harry Maxwell psychologist". Finger shaking, vibrating above the enter key. He closed his eyes and hit it. Top result, the video thumbnail. Face right there, drunk as a fish, trousers round his ankles. Above his website, above his profiles, above it all. Hundreds of views. Refreshed, hundreds more. Refreshed again, thousands now. Smashed his finger against the refresh button, time and time again, watching the number grow, grow, grow.

Another client cancellation came in through an email—Jules Patrick. The redhead with the Romeo scam, the one who asked him out. The one who called him sweet.

"Can't see you anymore Harry. Thought you were different, better, but you're just like all the rest. Bye."

More views. Thousands of them. Thousands more with every refresh.

Harry watched in real-time as his entire life was dismantled, notification by notification. Years of building trust, reputation, relationships—all destroyed in minutes.

His phone rang. Tim.

"Harry mate, what the fuck." Tim's voice was cold, controlled fury. "My boys saw this, Harry. My children. Steve's only six, and he's asking me why Uncle Harry doesn't have his trousers on. What did you fucking do?"

"Tim, please, I can explain—"

"Explain what? That you're a pervert? That you whip your cock out to strangers on the internet? Jesus Christ, Harry mate, what the fuck is wrong with you?"

"It's not what it looks like. I was scammed, Tim. Someone recorded me—"

"I don't want to hear it Harry. Damage is done. Just steer clear mate—steer clear."

The line went dead.

Harry tried calling back immediately, but Tim had blocked his number. His own brother poisoned against him.

More calls came in. Clients cancelling appointments. Journalists wanting statements. Someone claiming to be from a gossip blog asking for an interview. Harry let them all go to voicemail.

The video had thousands more views, dozens of shares, countless crude comments from strangers. Someone had even made memes using screenshots of his face.

Crystal clear quality. His identity unmistakable. No plausible deniability. Undeniably, irreversibly him.

His phone continued buzzing with notifications, each one another nail in the coffin of his reputation, his life.

His brother, his friends, his professional standing, his business—all destroyed because he'd trusted someone he'd never actually met. All those clients, all those scams, and yet he still fell face first into the trap.

The medieval imagery that had brought him joy now haunted him. He wasn't a knight—he was a disgraced jester, stripped of dignity before a jeering crowd.

His world was crumbling and all he could do was cry, slumped over his mahogany desk.

The worst part was knowing that somewhere out there, Harriet was watching this unfold and enjoying every second of his suffering. Whoever she was, whatever her reasons—she must really, really hate him.

Harry sat motionless, staring at the phone. It had stopped buzzing now. Or maybe he just stopped hearing it. Same thing.

Desk didn't feel smooth, or comforting, or earned anymore. Just a lump of wood.

Clock ticked, tolled in his ears. Tick. Tock. Tick. Tock.

Chapter 36

Harry spent the next three days in bed, crying, clutching Mr Snuffles to his chest, a shield against the darkness.

He'd texted Olivia Monday telling her she had the week off. That was the last time he looked at his phone, notifications now presumably in their hundreds, if not more.

He wanted to visit his aunt, but didn't. She wouldn't recognise him, but the staff certainly would.

He was famous now, just like fake Harriet said.

Thursday arrived. Harry made note of the time and decided to take a chance.

His reputation ruined, future uncertain, business in tatters—but if he could talk to his brothers in arms, his brother in blood—maybe he could salvage something.

Anything.

He rushed to the church, kit bag ready. He wasn't sure why he'd prepared his gear—they weren't likely to hug and make up, then get straight back to sparring. But if they could just hear him out—maybe the society would survive.

Simon stood at the door, arms folded, disapproving glare fixed on Harry as he approached.

"Simon, please. I—"

"Key."

Simon interrupted, gesturing for Harry to hand over the church keys.

"Wait, what? But I—"

Simon gestured "zip it" and beckoned again for the key.

This didn't feel fair. He wouldn't even hear him out.

Harry could see Tim furiously polishing his helmet inside, and Jester moping in the corner, avoiding eye contact.

Simon glared, growing impatient. Harry reluctantly handed over the key. Simon nodded.

"Can I talk to my brother? Please, let me explain."

Simon sighed and shook his head, gesturing towards Harry's car. His meaning was clear—leave.

Tim didn't want to talk. Harry had known from the blocked number, but it stung worse in person.

He could have tried reasoning with Simon, but it seemed pointless. He was lost to them now, an outcast.

The group was all he had. His best friends, through thick and thin. The practice, his soon to dwindle savings—nothing compared to losing his medieval society.

Tears formed as he turned toward his car. Simon stepped back inside, key in hand, closing the doors with a boom that reverberated through Harry's soul.

He'd never been more lonely. All he had left was the judgmental glare of Mr Snuffles. He opened his car door, desperate to leave.

"Harry!"

Harry paused, turning to see Olivia running across the car park in her ornate armour. She still looked incredible.

"Why can't you join us? What's going on, Harry?"

Her genuine concern almost broke him as he rubbed tears from his eyes. Perhaps she hadn't seen his shame yet.

"You should go back inside, Olivia. I'm not welcome anymore."

"I don't understand. Simon is sad, but he wouldn't tell me why. Tim looked furious, and Jester wouldn't even look at me when I asked." She stepped closer, eyes filled with confusion. "Harry, you're scaring me. What's happening?"

Harry looked at this young woman—barely more than a girl, really—who'd somehow become the one constant in his crumbling world. How could he explain?

"I messed up, Olivia. The sort of thing that ruins friendships and reputations." His voice cracked. "You should stay away. For your own good."

"Don't be ridiculous." Olivia set her helmet down and reached out to touch his arm. "Whatever this is, whatever you think you've done—I don't care. You're the best man I know, Harry."

The warmth in her voice broke him. She was willing to stand by him when his brothers had exiled him.

"You don't understand, Olivia. When you find out what's happened, you'll feel differently."

"Then tell me. Let me decide for myself. I'm with you, Harry. I'm yours."

Harry shook his head, unable to meet her gaze. "I can't. Not here, not now."

Olivia stepped closer, close enough that he could smell strawberries beneath the metallic scent of her armour.

"Harry, look at me." When he didn't comply, she gently lifted his chin with her gauntleted hand. "Whatever this is, you don't have to face it alone. I'm here for you. I'll always be here for you. Look at me—see me. I'm right here, Harry, like I always have been."

The sincerity in her voice cracked his fragile shell. After brutal rejection from everyone who mattered, she offered unconditional support.

"Why?" he whispered. "Why stand by me?"

Olivia smiled—the same warm expression she'd worn countless times bringing him cinnamon swirls or a cheeky Chinese takeaway.

"I always have and always will, Harry Maxwell."

As the church doors remained firmly shut and the sound of swords grew fainter, Harry realised that Olivia might be the only person left who still believed in him.

The only person who still cared.

Chapter 37

Friday arrived whether Harry wanted it or not. Time kept ticking, it didn't stop for his misery.

No clients booked—nothing but cancellations. With Olivia taking the week off, nobody was manning the office phone. He considered updating the answerphone with some explanation, but what was the point? Nobody wanted to hear it.

This was the end. Without income, he couldn't pay office rent, bills, Olivia's wages. The business was finished, one fell swoop and everything he'd worked for would be gone.

The debts would crush him. His aunt's care, the house—everything.

Tim had warned him to steer clear, completely shunned him. Harry couldn't blame him—the thought of his nephews seeing that video was another dagger in the ribs.

He'd been in bed for half the day, hanging on to Mr Snuffles for dear life.

Harry checked his phone. Dozens more notifications—and a text from Olivia.

> *"Harry, I saw the video. It'll be OK. I'm here for you. You shouldn't be alone—come see me, please?"*

She was so thoughtful. Always watching over him, professionally and personally. Nobody knew him better—not Tim, not the medieval society, nobody.

Professional boundaries seemed insignificant now. The business was finished anyway.

> *"Sorry, Olivia. I appreciate you standing by me. I'm just not up for anything right now. Don't want to leave the house."*

Harry put his phone down, covered his head with his pillow. The sounds of life outside felt like mockery.

An hour passed. Two. Then another message arrived. From fake Harriet.

What could she possibly want? She'd completed her destruction, he had nothing left to lose. Everything, exactly as she'd said.

> *"Harry, darling. What fun we've had together! You're famous. I find myself a little bored now, though. Think I should go after that cute little secretary of yours next? Imagine her petite little naked body going through that same treatment as you, Harry. Oh darling, I'm excited just thinking about it! Let's make her a star, shall we?"*

This monster wasn't satisfied with destroying him— she wanted Olivia next. If she could devastate Harry with all his experience, was Olivia safe? How deep did Harriet's reach go?

Harry closed his eyes, breathed deep. Counted to ten until he regained composure.

Olivia would have her warning. A call felt insufficient—he distrusted his phone now. Harriet seemed to know exactly when to strike. She was watching him, listening to him, judging him just like the gulls outside.

The threat held merit. Olivia had mentioned the dating app before, he was sure. Harriet could be targeting her right now, posing as her perfect man.

He barely had the will to throw on clean clothes, but he had the will to warn Olivia.

After stopping for petrol—cosmic humour that his car had ran out now—he arrived at the run-down block of flats. Cracking bricks, broken roof tile still smashed on the floor.

He couldn't remember which door was hers. Had to concentrate, think about the address on payslips. It felt like years since he'd been here last.

Olivia must have heard the car. She came into the hallway and threw her arms around him.

The hug gave him no qualms—he needed it. He held her back, resisting the urge to cry into her shoulder.

"You came, Harry! Come in, sit down. Want a drink? Anything at all?"

She brought him inside, sat him on the sofa. Her pictures—lacking family—stared from the wall, same as before. Her flat was a shrine to loneliness, just like his home.

She sat beside him, arm around his shoulder, strawberry scents dancing in his nostrils.

"Harry, you seem upset. Is this about the video?"

Harry sat up straight, remembering why he'd come.

"Olivia! Listen. The scammer who blackmailed me— she's threatening you now. Please be careful—you could be talking to her now. Aren't you on the dating app?"

Olivia smiled and shook her head.

"No Harry, I haven't used it in ages. They just weren't right. They weren't you."

Harry's eyes widened. What was that?

Olivia gently touched his chin, turned his face toward her.

"I love you, Harry. What happened doesn't matter—we'll get past it. I've always been here for you, loved you like a woman, not an employee. Will you finally see me?"

Harry looked into her eyes, her confident yet quivering lips.

The pictures on the wall told the story. She did love him, had for some time, and her smile up there told him that. His strict boundaries, concerns about their age difference—none of it would have allowed him to see this.

He'd had to lose everything to see how much she loved him. And he loved her, too. But his concerns needed voicing.

"Olivia... I do love you. But I'm twice your age, almost. I don't have much to offer anymore. My business is done, I may lose my home—I'm not sure this can work."

Olivia interrupted with a deep, passionate kiss. Hungry, wanting, needy—yet hasty, inexperienced.

"Semantics, Harry. We'll figure it all out. But you're finally here. Finally mine."

Olivia stood and grinned before pulling off her shirt, tossing it carelessly on the floor, hands on her hips.

This didn't feel completely right, but it wasn't wrong either. Something about seeing Olivia stood there felt strangely familiar as the strawberry scents lingered still.

She reached out her hand. Harry held it back as a flood of emotion struck him, like the waves crashing against the shore. He rose, and she led him down the narrow hall, past the pictures, to her bedroom.

Chapter 38

Harry lay in bed next to Olivia, staring into the cosmos on the ceiling, hands behind his head.

He was broken, but happy. Incomplete, yet whole. All was right in this room, when all was wrong around him.

He didn't know the ethical ramifications of this. For the moment, he didn't care. All the petty issues and insecurities evaporated in Olivia's arms, at least for the time being.

"Harry, that was wonderful. Exactly how I wanted my first time to be!"

Olivia hugged him tight, kissing him on the cheek as he continued staring into the cosmos, strawberry scents lingering in his nose.

"I'll go shower. I think we should order takeaway after—my treat?"

Harry was tempted. He hadn't eaten a proper meal in days, his grumbling stomach reminding him.

"I think we're both out of work now, Olivia. You sure we can afford it?"

"Yep! My treat. I'll go shower, then sort us pizza."

Olivia blew him a kiss, posing naked for just a moment, before heading for the en suite bathroom.

In a way, he was lucky. He'd lost everything, but he had his health, his life, and Olivia. Something still nagged at him, though. A feeling of unease, even dread.

The soothing sound of cascading water running across Olivia's skin before striking the shower floor calmed him a little. He sat up, pulled on his clothes and sat on her side of the bed.

A notification flashed up on Olivia's phone, carelessly left on the bedside table. He didn't mean to pry, his eyes drawn to the light.

'Harriet, your subscription has expired'

The blood in Harry's veins turned to acid. His heart began beating out of his chest.

Harriet.

Longsword, heavy in his hands. Her eyes on him, as he drew it for the first time, blade gleaming in the moonlight. Perfectly forged for him—not a gift, a shackle.

Harriet.

Takeaway, on his desk, craved it for days. Spring rolls, fried rice. "I know you so well, Harry." Kindness? Cataloguing. Pavlov's dog. He was shaking. Vibrating, almost.

Harriet.

Tent in the dark, her voice a whisper, strawberry scent choking him. "Can you finally see me, Harry?" Not hope, not vulnerability, not friendship—Hunger, wearing the mask of longing.

Breathe, Harry. Breathe. In, and out. He closed his eyes, steeling himself for the shower to stop. He had to get out—now. He needed to be alone, needed to think. He desperately, frantically searched for a tie to straighten, finding only fear.

Harriet.

With a small, metallic creak, the shower stopped, the cascade of water ceased. The bell had tolled—she would soon make her approach.

Olivia stepped back into the bedroom, wrapped in a towel. She came over and kissed him on the cheek. Her lips felt like acid, her love felt like hate. She had betrayed him, abused him, manipulated him and destroyed him—totally, cruelly and completely. Five little careless words was all it took to know. So simple in her downfall, so careless, so human.

But he couldn't focus on that yet. He had to leave, and he had to do it now.

"Pizza time?" Olivia asked, reaching for her phone, as Harry forced a smile masking the screaming, fraying nerves.

"I need to go, actually. This whole situation has left me busier than ever, even with no clients."

Olivia's bubbly smile quickly turned to a scowl.

"But that's not fair! We were going to have dinner, and I wanted to have sex again. Besides, you're home now. Where are you going?"

Olivia folded her arms and glared at Harry, studying him like a textbook.

Harry forced down bile.

"Just home, Olivia. I've been through a lot. Where's that kind, compassionate Olivia we know and love? I'm going back for tonight."

He wanted to explode. He needed to leave. Now.

Olivia softened a little.

"Can I join you, then?" she said suggestively.

"Come for breakfast. We'll have quite the day together tomorrow, I'm sure."

Harry kissed her on the cheek, betraying the rage and pain screaming in his brain, the walls as tight as his chest.

Olivia smiled, hands back on her hips.

"All right, Harry! Well, that's fine. I'm sure you need some space. But not before round two?"

Olivia beckoned to the bed, grinning.

Oh God. There was no way. He'd rather jump off the promenade into the ocean, wearing stylish concrete shoes.

"Sorry, Olivia—man my age? That'll have to wait until breakfast."

Olivia slumped but wasn't entirely unsympathetic.

"Maybe you are too old after all, Harry. Ha! All right, my love. A breakfast date it is. I'm off to the shower—to think about you some more. Love you!"

Another kiss on his cheek, another dose of acid searing his skin.

He waved and smiled, wiping his cheek as she went back to the en suite.

Time to get the hell out of there.

Chapter 39

Harry wasn't safe to drive, but he had no choice. He was shaking, violently convulsing, his body and mind poised to implode. He concentrated hard on the road ahead, hum of the tyres the only thing keeping him sane.

He didn't make it home, but he made it far enough from the grotty flat to be safe from the monster. From Olivia. From fake Harriet.

He got out and violently threw up by the roadside. Mostly bile.

Harry slumped back in the driver's seat, a complete mess of warbling tears. He couldn't think about this yet— he had to breathe, focus, reach home.

One excruciating drive complete, Harry stumbled through his front door to the familiar smell of home, the judgemental silence bar the gentle hum of the fridge.

He locked the door and placed a kitchen chair against it in case the monster tried to barge in, and demolish his home—like she'd demolished his entire life.

He ran upstairs, grabbed Mr Snuffles and cried. Cried hard, cried fierce until there were no tears left.

Still shaking, he breathed in deep, counting to ten, time and time again.

He pictured Olivia dancing around her living room, eating pizza, whilst he quivered like a child who'd witnessed a brutal murder.

Pizza she'd eat while celebrating his destruction. The life she'd stolen. The life she'd ruined just to swoop in as his saviour once destruction was complete.

Starting to calm—at least enough to think—so many things began making sense.

Olivia's constant encroachment on his personal life. Her need for inclusion and control. The amateur yet professional way she'd gained leverage to destroy him.

Breath in. Ten seconds, breathe out. Detach. Analyse.

Foster care revelation. Vulnerable, isolated, needed protecting. Textbook, mark to rescuer. Boundaries to burdens, distance to guilt.

Stomach lurched. Swallowed hard.

Brothers in Steel. Accidentally stumbled onto it through an advert? No. Researched. Engineered proximity, not fate. No coincidences, only designs.

Food. All his favourites, all his comforts, timed and served to perfection. Pavlov's dog, her presence felt comfy, his stomach her ward.

Hands, shaking. Breathe in. Ten. Out.

Harriet and The Matrix. Calculated intoxication. Perfect trap, sprung with expert precision. Never stood a chance.

Coldness, last week. Post-event blues? No. Strategy. Withdraw affection, create anxiety, desperation to restore approval. Only person left who wanted him. Isolation and dependence.

All textbook. All obvious. To everyone but him.

In her twisted young mind, maybe she truly thought she loved him. The manipulative, possessive version of love that exists in adolescent fantasy.

Nobody who loved him could do this. This wasn't love. This was manipulation, extortion, control.

Everything made sense now. The level of access Olivia had, her complete knowledge of his working and personal life. All that time studying—IT courses, psychology books, his own published works—the scam itself, feeling so professional yet amateur. It was targeted—a deeply personal sextortion scam designed to lure him directly into her arms.

That familiar feeling he'd got from the start, like he and Harriet were old friends. She already knew everything about him. Had there been clues he'd missed? Were there signs, warnings, slips in her mask all along?

It didn't matter. The damage was done, his life in shambles, and it would never read the same again.

Harriet, your subscription has expired. The five words that brought her scheme low. Her victory so absolute, her triumph so complete, she didn't even care. Arrogance. Immaturity.

He had to focus. The truth was out—to him, at least. He'd hoped Olivia's carelessness extended to not noticing his state when he left, but someone who studied him so intently could have noticed anything.

If she suspected he'd seen the notification, what would it change? He'd still lost everything. Now, even her.

He still couldn't get his head round this. Sweet, helpful Olivia, always wanting to support him, bringing his favourite foods. All that care, yet this?

She'd treated him like a complete and utter fool.

But Harry Maxwell was a counsellor, not a fool. The biggest mistake he'd ever made was taking a chance on hiring a girl called Olivia.

He began to feel paranoid—every noise, every tick of the clock out to get him.

Breathe in. Ten. Breathe out.

A plan was forming. He had nothing left to lose, his life decimated. Olivia would have her breakfast date—but Harry needed a trip to the office first.

Chapter 40

Harry barely slept that night. Staring at the ceiling, seething with quiet rage. He flitted between blaming himself and blaming Olivia. Hating himself, and hating her.

He checked his phone. The missed calls, notifications, texts and emails had slowed, but they were still coming.

A text from Olivia:

> *"Morning handsome. You up and ready for breakfast? What are you making? Olivia x"*

Ready? Not even remotely. But ready or not, the show must go on.

> *"Head on over, bus should be coming your way in ten. See you soon, darling."*

He got up and prepared himself. The works today—shower, full clean shave, suit and tie. Harry Maxwell had a new client, and he intended to treat her with the same compassion and respect as any other.

His hands shook as he tightened his blue silk tie. Couldn't get it to sit right, but it would have to do. He looked almost normal—professional, suited and booted, ready for his next session. Only his hollow eyes gave him away.

Everything.

He headed downstairs, fired up his hob and got cooking. Full English breakfast, fried eggs, sausages, baked beans—the works. More than enough for two. An old friend once gave him a tip that good food puts clients at ease, talk freely, drop their guard.

Olivia. Every little cinnamon swirl, every Chinese takeaway, every macaroni cheese and pizza appearing exactly when he needed it. Good food made good company.

Two eggs, cracked against the pan. Hands steadier, but the shake still there. Eggs sizzling in his ears. Still couldn't shake that strawberry scent from his mind, or his soul.

Focus on cooking. Sausages. Pricked, browned, precise.

Transcription device hung on his keyring, small black plastic catching the morning light. Green light, ready to roll. Tested it twice. Cloud storage active, recording to the server in real-time. They had a plan, and he would be ready for it. Do as they said, get her talking, let her explain.

Plated the food thoughtfully, arranged the food in a smile, with the two eggs and the bacon. Appealing and symmetrical, loving and disarming.

Was this ethical? Entrapment? Illegal, even? Thoughts raced as he stared at the little green light.

Ethics meant nothing to her. Nothing at all. All ash, because he closed his eyes one time too many.

One last client session with his most challenging manipulator yet. Felled by her own arrogance, her immature assumption she had him hook, line and sinker. Just a silly little app notification. So mundane, so simple, so perfect.

Table set. Cutlery, neat and perfect.

Everything.

Fervent little taps on his front door signalled Olivia's arrival.

Deep breath, count to ten, open up. Showtime.

"Morning, Olivia. Come sit, I've made a full English." Harry gestured towards the wooden table at the centre of the kitchen, adorned with the feast.

She didn't need telling twice. Her face lit up as she rushed over and helped herself, scoffing down the meal before her.

Once replete, she relaxed back in her chair, staring intently at Harry sat across from her.

"That was delicious, Harry. Should have got you to cook at work. I love your new pet name for me—your darling. Where'd you get that?"

Olivia smiled, gazing lovingly at Harry as he studied her, elbows firmly on the table, hands clasped tightly.

"From you, Harriet."

Silence.

Olivia's eyes began to twinkle. She quickly grimaced a smile, calculating her reply.

"It's Olivia, silly. Who's Harriet? Do I need to be jealous, Harry?"

Harry smiled.

"You already asked me that. When you were posing as Harriet. Drop it, Olivia. I know. It's over."

Olivia began hyperventilating, panicking, breathing fast and shallow, tears rolling down her cheeks.

"Harry! Please, I—I can explain! Just listen!"

Harry stared at her, his heart sinking. They were not the tears of a crocodile, and the care she showed was genuine. A twisted, malevolent kind of love, but she did love him, as he did her.

"There was always something familiar about the way you scammed me, Olivia. Right from the first moment you messaged me as Harriet, I felt a connection, like I was talking to an old friend. It gave me hope, purpose, dreams of a future, of a family. Like Tim, Yvette and the boys. The family you stole from me when you destroyed my reputation."

"You did this, Harry. No matter what I did, you just didn't see me. Didn't notice me. I love you, Harry! Why couldn't you have just seen that from the start? Why did you make me do this to you?"

Harry sighed, hands flat on the table. Stared at her for a long moment as the seconds stretched.

"There's some truth to your madness, Olivia."

"Wait, what?"

She seemed almost surprised by his admission.

"The way you took care of me, the attention you showed me, the support and affection...I loved it. I told myself it was unprofessional, but I let those lines between us blur. What you did, it was cruel, callous, vicious. But I should have seen the signs, and should have been firm with you. I am not entirely to blame, but neither are you."

Olivia wiped away her tears and hardened her gaze.

"Don't you get it, Harry? When I found her, I saw your perfect match. But she's no different to me! Just older and has the doctorate. I'm your perfect match, Harry, and I always was!"

Tears sneaked out of Harry's eyes. Too stubborn, too 'professional' to ever see it, but it was no lie. The family he wanted had been waiting for him all along, but now, he sat across from the ashes.

"I would never have let myself see it, not as I was. And you? You just wouldn't let it go, would you? Even now?"

Olivia's eyes fixed firmly on his throat.

"You did this, Harry. No matter what I did, you just didn't see me. Didn't notice me. I love you, Harry! Why couldn't you have just seen that from the start? Why did you make me do this to you?"

"Oh Olivia, you really believe that? I didn't make you do anything. But how did you even do it, anyway? The academic email, perfectly copying the real Dr Baker, how?"

Olivia sobbed hard, quivering.

"I... I set up a redirect on your email. When you emailed her academic email it went to me. There was so much public footage of her, I could use it to clone her perfectly with the deepfake software. I had to make her, to make you see me, Harry! Don't you see that?"

Keep talking, Olivia. Keep sharing, my love.

"You recorded me exposed on camera, Olivia. You blackmailed me with that video. You destroyed my entire life—my reputation, my business, my relationships with everyone I care about. All because of your purported love? Is that how people who love each other behave, Olivia?"

Olivia shook her head furiously.

"Harry, please! I did it for us! Don't you see? You never would have chosen me otherwise. You were so stubborn, so blind to what was right in front of you. I had to make you see—"

"Wait." Olivia's gaze darted around the kitchen and landed on an all too familiar gadget. A little black device, designed as a keyring, hanging from the car keys above his kitchen sink.

The green light on the transcription device, indicating it was recording. That their conversation was being transcribed in full text and recorded in audio too.

Lovely little thing really. Helped Harry keep track of all his clients, including his most challenging one yet.

Olivia stood without missing a beat and grabbed the keys from the hook. She dropped them on the floor, device included, stomping on it fervently until it was destroyed, shattered into broken pieces across the kitchen tiles.

Precisely as she'd so carelessly done with his entire life.

Harry frowned as tears fell from Olivia's face. A coldness returned to her gaze as she trained it on him.

"That takes care of that. You are mine, Harry. No more recordings or transcriptions. I own you. I have demands."

Harry raised an eyebrow.

"I'll use that software again. I worked hard, Harry. I can create anything I want. You're going to marry me, Harry. And I want a baby. No, I want two, like your brother has."

A dagger in Harry's ribs. A beautiful dream, wrapped around a nightmare. No going back now. He gazed at her, longing, crying, shaking his head.

"I'm serious, Harry! This is happening!"

Harry wiped his eyes and took a deep breath.

"I'm sorry, Olivia. I truly do want a wife, a family, my little Chester and Emily. In another world, it could—no, should—have been you. Been us. But I don't think we're going to be able to maintain the passion with you in jail now, are we?"

Olivia had forgotten something important. The transcription device recorded directly to cloud storage, accessible only to herself and Harry.

Herself, Harry, and DCI Peters, who Harry had had the pleasure of an hour-long interview with first thing this morning. Lovely chap, very professional.

"Careless, Olivia. Just like the app notification on your phone. So completely ignorant in your moment of triumph, you forgot something important. I love you, Olivia, and I think I always will. But now, I think it's time for your next appointment—don't you, 'darling'?"

Olivia screamed and threw her fork at him, then her plate, then her knife. Lucky he'd only given her a butter knife with her breakfast.

Still, she had a full day ahead of her. Least he could do was feed her a decent meal for her impending stay under the gentle care of the Norfolk Constabulary.

"This isn't over, Harry. I'll tell them things. I'll make up things. You are mine. MINE!"

Hearing the yelling, two uniformed officers quickly entered via the front door and arrested Olivia.

The silence that followed as they drove her away seemed almost oppressive. He missed her already, her absence gnawing, longing.

Harry had won—but at what cost?

Epilogue

Over a year had passed since that fateful day.

Hard times for Harry. Business folded, professional reputation in tatters. He'd found a one-bedroom flat to rent in the nearby town of King's Lynn.

Harry had grown out a beard and shaved his head. At first, to help hide his face, distance himself from the blackmail video that had ruined his life. Over time, as the story became old news, he'd grown rather fond of the new look.

"Welcome, everyone. Good to see you all here. Seems we have a newcomer—what's your name?" Harry asked, sitting on his plastic chair, facing the newest member of his group.

Harry had a new start, hired as a group counsellor for domestic abuse victims. Once his story was old news, it seemed fitting somehow. A tough job, with abuse often being physical as well as psychological, but he understood their plight as they did his.

The little church hall they sat in was overly bright with fluorescent lights, not particularly welcoming. The plastic chairs weren't exactly comfortable either.

But Harry provided snacks for the clients, met with great enthusiasm. He swore Sandra showed up just to deprive him of his cinnamon swirls.

"Hi, I'm, uh, I'm Paul," stuttered the newest addition to Harry's little flock.

Harry opened his arms and welcomed him to the group. Mostly women, but there were one or two men as well, himself included.

An hour went by in a blink. Tales of woe, love and loss, trial and tribulation shared amongst the group. Tears were spilled, hugs were given, and they packed up to leave, to be repeated next week.

Harry had to hurry, though. It was Thursday night, and he had somewhere to be.

An entire year since he'd seen the sea, since he'd filled his lungs with that fresh, salty air that gave him sustenance like a Sunday roast.

The drive was peaceful. Swapping one church for another, Harry had arrived.

The van was there, Simon and Jester presumably inside. Most importantly, Tim's car was there too.

They'd all be inside by now. Harry armoured up outside, save for his helmet, which he carried under his arm.

He took a deep breath, counted to ten, and pushed open the creaky church doors, the clanging of steel echoing biblically inside.

He didn't expect them to be happy to see him, but after all this time, didn't think they'd hate him either.

They all noticed his presence simultaneously, the creaky door announcing his arrival.

Whatever skirmish he'd walked in on stopped instantly. All eyes on him.

"Harry, mate? Is that you?"

Tim was first to speak, barely recognising his brother. He walked over, removing his helmet and placing it on a pew.

The animosity seemed distant now. Tim rushed over and threw his arms around Harry, tears welling in his eyes.

"I saw the news, mate. We all did. Olly, off to jail—we didn't realise. We had no idea. I tried to reach you, to find you—your number was disconnected, your Facebook deleted—mate, I—"

"It's all right," Harry interrupted, though he knew it never would be. Not fully—not truly.

Two years, she got. Two years for the life he built. Wasn't enough, but was something. Yet, he missed her, mourned her the entire time. Still loved her, even now, even after everything.

Simon walked over and offered his hand, smile on his face.

"Yo, Harry! I read your book. Jesus, man, Olivia was really messed up. Can't believe you stuck your dick in that bruv! Gross!"

Same old Jester.

"Bring it next time, I'll sign it for you. Well, if there is a next time, of course. Brothers in steel, I'm here to request something of you," Harry announced.

"Name it, mate. Name it."

Harry smiled, placing his helmet on his head, drawing his old viking broadsword Tim bought him all those years ago.

"A duel. A duel between brothers, to reclaim my honour and my place in the group. Fight me, Tim, and don't go easy on me. I'll know."

The three of them looked at one another, grins wide on their faces.

"Deal. Right then, Harry," Tim said, fastening the strap under his helmet, Jester standing to marshal.

Not to reclaim what was lost, that was impossible—but forging something new from the ashes.

"Let's duel."

Printed in Dunstable, United Kingdom